"*A Girl's Guide to the Wild* prepares a girl not only for the outdoors but also for planning, executing, and enjoying any goal of her young life. This essential book is for every kid who dreams of an outdoor adventure and for the worried parents who want to help."

—**CAROLINE PAUL**, author of *The Gutsy Girl: Escapades for Your Life of Epic Adventure*

"Just the thing to help girls get comfortable in the outdoors or encourage the interest of those who want to learn more!"

—**LIBBY RIDDLES**, first woman to win the Iditarod

"Full of terrific ideas, practical tips, and inspiring stories, *A Girl's Guide to the Wild* is a must read for every young adventurer."

—**RICHARD LOUV**, author of *Last Child in the Woods*, *The Nature Principle*, and *Vitamin N*

A girl's guide to the Wild

BE AN ADVENTURE-SEEKING OUTDOOR EXPLORER!

RUBY McCONNELL

illustrations by TERESA GRASSESCHI

little bigfoot

an imprint of sasquatch books
seattle, wa

NOTE TO PARENTS: Many outdoor (and indoor) activities pre-
sented in this book have risks associated with them. Nothing in this
book should be attempted without proper and professional
training and supervision. Neither the author nor the publisher
assumes any responsibility for any injuries incurred by the reader.
Maps included in this book are not intended to be used for navigation.

Printed in the United States of America

LITTLE BIGFOOT with colophon is a registered trademark of
Penguin Random House LLC

23 22 21 20 19   9 8 7 6 5 4 3 2 1

Editor: Hannah Elnan | Production editor: Bridget Sweet
Design: Anna Goldstein | Illustrations: Teresa Grasseschi

Library of Congress Cataloging-in-Publication Data
Names: McConnell, Ruby, author.
Title: A girl's guide to the wild : be an adventure-seeking outdoor explorer!
  / Ruby McConnell.
Description: Seattle : Little Bigfoot, [2019] | Audience: 9-12 | Includes
  bibliographical references and index.
Identifiers: LCCN 2018028567 | ISBN 9781632171719 (pbk.)
Subjects: LCSH: Outdoor recreation for women. | Outdoor recreation for
  children.
Classification: LCC GV191.64 .M42 2019 | DDC 796.082--dc23
LC record available at https://lccn.loc.gov/2018028567

ISBN: 978-1-63217-171-9

Sasquatch Books
1904 Third Avenue, Suite 710
Seattle, WA 98101
SasquatchBooks.com

Certified Chain of Custody
SUSTAINABLE Promoting Sustainable Forestry
FORESTRY
INITIATIVE   www.sfiprogram.org
              SFI-01268

SFI label applies to the text stock

For Paul, who takes me to the woods

Contents

Part 3

ADVANCED SKILLS   157

PROJECTS

· · · · · · · · · · · · · · · · ·

RECIPES

· · · · · · · · · · · · · · ·

WHY GO OUTSIDE?

Before the 1950s, most people in the United States lived on farms or in rural, small towns. For them, being outside was a part of daily life. Now, most people live in cities or suburban areas, where there is less space without buildings, paved roads, and the sounds of engines. But there's a whole world of adventure out there waiting to be explored, and it's filled with miles-high mountaintops, ancient forests, hidden caves, northern lights—things you can't experience from inside a building, along a city street, or through any kind of screen.

This book is all about *doing*: going outside, playing games, learning new skills, hiking, biking, climbing, cooking, and so much more. Remember, big adventures come with risks and rewards, so before you get started, make sure that you learn (and follow) the *Girl's Guide* Rules of the Wild.

RULES OF THE WILD

1. Ask permission.
2. Make a plan.
3. Collect the right tools.

4. Keep a positive attitude.
5. Help others.
6. Do no harm.

PART 1

So, You Want to Go Outside

CHAPTER 1

PLACES NEAR AND FAR

Oh, give me land, lots of land, and the starry skies above,

Don't fence me in.

—ROBERT FLETCHER AND COLE PORTER

You don't have to travel very far to get outdoors; you can start your adventures right in your own backyard, school grounds, or a local city park. Many cities have parks that are big enough to hike or even camp in. Once you build your skills, you can look for adventures farther from home. Ask your family members or friends where they like to go hiking or camping or check out a guidebook on local hikes from the public library.

TRY THIS! Sign up for a nature or outdoor program at a local park.

NATIONAL PARKS AND FORESTS

For a bigger adventure, explore one of the many national parks and forests that have been set aside for all of us to enjoy. The National Park Service was created in 1916 to showcase and protect the most interesting, jaw-dropping, and beautiful places in the United States, including the deepest lake, one of the largest volcanoes in the world, and the only tropical forest in the United States. The first park was Yellowstone National Park, in Wyoming, Montana, and Idaho. Today, there are sixty national parks spread out across the country. The biggest is Wrangell–St. Elias National Park and Preserve, in Alaska; it's 2,166 times larger than the smallest, Hot Springs National Park, in Arkansas!

The largest areas used for outdoor recreation in the United States are the national forests. Like the national parks, these are big areas of land set aside for recreation, but they are also used for industry, agriculture, and natural resources and are much larger than national parks. Many of the national forests aren't forests at all! Some of these areas are grasslands and deserts without a tree in sight. Part of the purpose of the US Forest Service, which manages these lands, is to protect and preserve our water and other natural resources for future generations. It is also in charge of preventing and putting out forest fires. There are national forests in forty-one of the fifty states. Together, they make up an area the size of Texas! Forest Service land and all 154 national forests are owned by everyone, including you. That means that we *all* have the opportunity to experience and enjoy them, but also the responsibility to protect them.

DID YOU KNOW? The Forest Service started using the character Smokey Bear to educate people about forest fires more than 75 years ago, after the movie *Bambi* brought attention to the problem of wildfires.

Ten Great National Parks

DENALI, ALASKA

Denali National Park is almost the same size as the entire state of New Hampshire but has only one road that runs through it! It is named for the highest mountain in the United States, Denali, whose peak is more than 20,000 feet tall, as high as some passenger airplanes fly.

YELLOWSTONE; WYOMING, MONTANA, AND IDAHO

Because Yellowstone National Park lies entirely within the *caldera* (crater) of a volcano, the park is spotted with hot springs and geysers. Yellowstone is also home to some of the largest wild buffalo and elk herds in the United States.

GLACIER, MONTANA

YELLOWSTONE;
WYOMING, MONTANA,
AND IDAHO

BADLANDS,
SOUTH DAKOTA

REDWOOD,
CALIFORNIA

GRAND CANYON, ARIZONA

DENALI, ALASKA

HAWAI'I VOLCANOES, HAWAI'I

SHENANDOAH,
VIRGINIA

GREAT SMOKY MOUNTAINS,
NORTH CAROLINA AND TENNESSEE

EVERGLADES, FLORIDA

GRAND CANYON, ARIZONA

The Grand Canyon is 190 miles long and more than a mile deep in some places. It covers more than 1,900 square miles—four times the size of Los Angeles! The rocks in the Grand Canyon are a record of close to 2 billion years of earth's natural history.

REDWOOD, CALIFORNIA

Redwood National Park protects some of the oldest and tallest trees remaining in the United States (including the California coast redwood, for which the park is named). Some of these trees are more than 3,000 years old!

GLACIER, MONTANA

Glacier, named for its abundant alpine ice sheets (glaciers), is the only national park to share an international border with another park; in 1932, Canada's Waterton Lakes National Park and Glacier were named the first international peace park in the world. Visit soon; climate change has melted more than half the park's iconic ice.

HAWAI'I VOLCANOES, HAWAI'I

Hawai'i Volcanoes National Park is home to Mauna Loa and Kilauea, some of the most active volcanoes in the world. At night, visitors can watch the lava's red glow from Kilauea's crater.

GREAT SMOKY MOUNTAINS, NORTH CAROLINA AND TENNESSEE

Great Smoky Mountains National Park is named for the blue mist that is formed from the evaporation of more than 80 inches of rain that falls annually onto the park's nearly 100 species of trees. It is also the world's salamander capital and one of the few national parks that are free to visit!

EVERGLADES, FLORIDA

Everglades National Park is the largest *mangrove ecosystem* (a massive forest of trees that sit directly in salty coastal waters) in the western hemisphere. The park is also an important source of water; it supplies one-third of Florida's drinking water!

BADLANDS, SOUTH DAKOTA

Badlands are areas of steeply eroded sedimentary rocks that form narrow canyons and rock pillars called *hoodoos*. The rocks that make up Badlands National Park contain some of the most abundant and diverse fossils in the world and show that the parklands once were home to the saber-toothed tiger.

SHENANDOAH, VIRGINIA

Shenandoah National Park is long and narrow, following the high peaks of the Blue Ridge Mountains. This park is known for its many hiking trails, including 101 miles of the Appalachian Trail (see page 15 for more on the Appalachian Trail), and its spectacular views of fall colors.

WORLD HERITAGE SITES

World Heritage sites are places that the *United Nations* (the world organization of governments) has recognized as being of special natural, scientific, or cultural importance. These sites include lost cities, palaces and castles, pyramids, epic statues, ancient ruins, and historic town centers. There are 203 World Heritage sites recognized just for their natural uniqueness, where some of the world's most interesting and fragile natural wonders can be found.

Ten Great World Heritage Sites

SERENGETI NATIONAL PARK AND NGORONGORO CONSERVATION AREA, TANZANIA

Serengeti and its neighbor Ngorongoro are the sites of the largest land-mammal migration in the world, with millions of wildebeests, zebras, giraffes, and other grassland animals crossing it annually. It is also home to one of the largest populations of wild lions in the world.

JASPER NATIONAL PARK, CANADA

Jasper is the largest of the Canadian Rocky Mountain Parks and is known for its views of the northern Rocky Mountains, waterfalls, and the Athabasca Glacier, the most visited glacier in North America.

MOUNT FUJI, JAPAN

Mount Fuji, Japan's tallest mountain, was named a World Heritage site in 2013, but unlike other sites listed here, it received the honor for cultural, rather than natural, reasons. The mountain, while beautiful and wild, received the honor for its contribution to Japan's culture and role in inspiring artists of all kinds.

CENTRAL AMAZON CONSERVATION COMPLEX, BRAZIL

This protected portion of the Amazon rain forest contains more species than almost any other place on earth and is home to the world's largest assortment of electric fish. This rain forest is an important source of clean air for the entire planet.

SURTSEY, ICELAND

Surtsey is a volcanic island like Hawai'i, but it emerged from beneath the ocean recently—in the mid-1960s. Surtsey has always been a protected area, so it serves as the world's most pristine laboratory for the study of how plants and animals migrate to newly formed land.

TASMANIAN WILDERNESS, AUSTRALIA

The Tasmanian Wilderness is one of the last large expanses of *temperate* (a mild climate) rain forest in the world, covering almost 20 percent of the island. While no people live there now, there is evidence of humans dating back nearly 20,000 years.

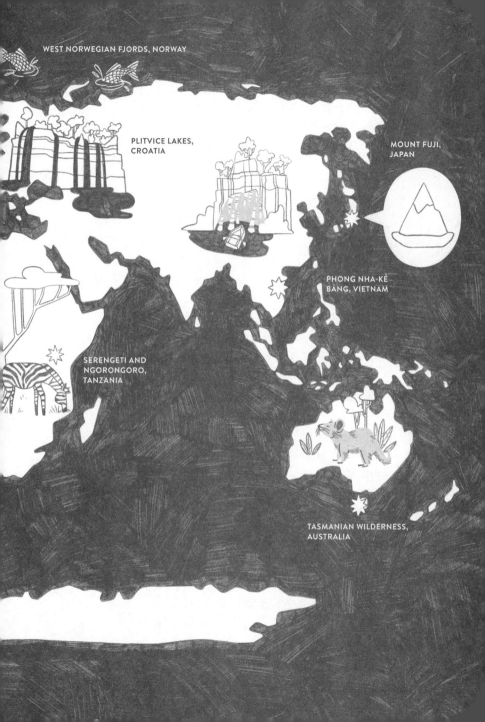

WEST NORWEGIAN FJORDS, NORWAY

Nærøyfjord and Geirangerfjord, two *fjords* in Norway, are considered the world's best (and biggest) examples of these unusual, steep-sided valleys. Fjords are formed when valley glaciers from high mountains flow into the sea.

PLITVICE LAKES, CROATIA

This Croatian national park consists of a series of sixteen lakes connected to each other by waterfalls that cascade into bright-blue pools. The water from the falls eventually flows into a large cavern.

PHONG NHA-KẾ BÀNG, VIETNAM

Phong Nha-Kẻ Bàng is one of the world's biggest *karst* areas (cave regions where water has dissolved limestone). There are over three hundred caves and stone grottos in the area that have been mapped, but large portions of the more than 80-mile-long cave system remain unexplored.

THE GALÁPAGOS ISLANDS, ECUADOR

The Galápagos Islands, in the Pacific Ocean, host the largest number of species unique to one place in the world. The islands were the inspiration for Charles Darwin's theory of evolution, which explains how living things change over time.

DID YOU KNOW? Some of the oldest living things in the world are in World Heritage sites. The seagrass surrounding the Balearic Islands of Spain is 100,000 years old!

TRY THIS! Find a national park or World Heritage site near you. How long does it take to get there? Do you have to drive, or can you take a different kind of transportation? How much does it cost to visit the site? What special things will you be able to see? Can you find a friend, parent, or mentor to take you?

LONGER TRIPS

. . . .

Some adventures last longer than a day or weekend—much longer. Some people take weeks to climb the highest mountains, sail around the world, or ride their bikes across an entire continent. There are lots of trails famous for long-distance journeys, some of which take you through abandoned ghost towns or are a part of history themselves, like the Great Wall of China. The Pacific Crest and Appalachian Trails both run the length of the United States from north to south. It can take up to six months to hike those trails! Longer trips require extra planning and training, so if you want to go on one of these epic adventures someday, practice your outdoor skills as often as you can and get plenty of exercise, so you stay healthy and strong.

Craft an Adventure Globe

You can record and share the memories you make and dream about where you want to go next by creating your own globe to document where you've been and where you want to go. Are you interested in mountains? Seeing wild animals? Beautiful beaches? Have you visited a forest or a national park? Mark your adventures!

WHAT YOU'LL NEED:

2 cups water
1 cup flour
2 tablespoons salt
Round balloon
Newspaper (torn or cut into 1- to 2-inch-wide strips that are 6 to 8 inches long)
Reference map (you can use the map of World Heritage sites on pages 12–13 or find a globe, world map, or internet map site)
Acrylic paint
Pencil or felt-tip markers
Stickers
Yarn
Glue

WHAT TO DO:

1. Make the papier-mâché paste by mixing two parts water (2 cups) to one part flour (1 cup) until it is free of lumps and about the same texture as pancake batter. Add the salt and mix again.

2. Blow up the balloon as big as you would like your globe to be.

3. Dredge the newspaper strips in papier-mâché paste and cover the balloon with three to four layers, allowing each layer to dry before adding the next. Let the entire globe dry for at least an hour, then pop the balloon.

4. Paint the globe blue and let it dry.

5. Using a globe or world map, lightly sketch the continents with a pencil or marker, then fill them in with paint.

6. Make a list of the places you have been and want to go to. Look up where they are on a globe, map of the world, or online.

7. Mark where you have been and at least five places you want to go with markers or stickers.

8. Cut the yarn into three equal pieces, and glue one end of each piece to the top of the globe, on the points of an imaginary triangle. Tie the three loose ends together to make a hanger for the globe.

ARUNIMA SINHA
Mountain Climber

Arunima Sinha was a national-level volleyball player in India when she lost her leg in a train accident. During her recovery, she became determined to find a new *junoon*, or passion: "I wanted to do something different—so different that everybody would say that it would be impossible." Inspired by stories of other female mountaineers, even before she was able to walk with her new prosthetic leg, she decided her *junoon* would be Mount Everest, the tallest land mountain in the world. Soon, the 23-year-old began training with the first Indian woman to summit Everest, learning new ways to move, carry, and climb. Less than 2 years later, after climbing for 52 days, she became the first woman amputee to summit Mount Everest, 60 years after the first mountaineers made it to the peak. Now, she is trying to summit the highest peaks on every continent to inspire girls of all ages and abilities to follow their dreams.

CHAPTER 2

GROUPS, TROOPS, AND SISTERHOODS

Say when, will we ever meet again?

Say when, dear friend, say when.

—CAMP SONG

The outdoors is a great place for friends, especially with an organized group. Groups can go farther, stay longer, and adventure harder together. There are outings for schools, sports teams, summer camps, and troops all designed to help you get outside. Some organizations, like 4-H, have regular meetings and schedule several trips a year, so that you can learn a variety of skills and sports and have plenty of chances to practice.

Summer camps have been one of the most popular ways to learn how to camp for over a hundred years. Some camps are for just a day or two, but other camps go on for weeks or even the whole summer.

Being in a group of just friends or family is special too. Having extra sets of hands makes packing, carrying, and cleanup tasks easier and more fun, and groups can also share gear and carpool. Most of all, traveling in a group lets you learn from others and gives you an opportunity to teach someone else your skills.

DID YOU KNOW? The first YWCA summer camp for girls was opened in 1874, 11 years before the first Boy Scout camp!

GREAT OUTDOOR TROOPS AND GROUPS

ALPENGIRL CAMP: Alpengirl Camp is a summer-camp program that takes all-girl groups, ages 11 to 16, on outdoor adventures throughout the western United States, including Olympic and Yellowstone National Parks. AlpengirlCamp.com

APPALACHIAN MOUNTAIN CLUB: Founded in 1876, the Appalachian Mountain Club is the oldest outdoor group in the United States. It has chapters from Maine to Washington, DC, and offers programs for school and youth groups as well as families. Outdoors.org

BETTIES360: Since 2005, Betties360 has offered free and low-cost adventure and action-sport opportunities to underserviced girls in and around Portland, Oregon, and is continuing to expand its program. Betties360.org

CAMP FIRE: Camp Fire was formed in 1910 as an all-girls alternative to the Boy Scouts, with the belief that girls, too, could benefit from learning outdoor skills. In fact, it was the first multiracial, multicultural, and nonreligious organization for girls in the United States. Today, it welcomes *all* kids. CampFire.org

CHEWONKI: Chewonki, based out of Maine, offers outdoor camps and leadership programs for a week or the whole summer for girls ages 8 to 16. Its programs include canoeing in Quebec and hiking the Maine Appalachian Trail. Chewonki.org

GIRL SCOUTS: The Girl Scouts is the oldest outdoor program for girls in the United States and has grown into an international organization that promotes self-reliance and skill building through community service and outdoor experiences for girls of all ages. GirlScouts.org

GIRLS QUEST: Girls Quest has spent the last 70 years working with low-income girls ages 8 to 17 in the New York area to build self-esteem and social skills through outdoor experiences. GirlsQuest.org

GIRLVENTURES: GirlVentures, based out of San Francisco, California, offers summer and after-school outdoor adventure opportunities to adolescent girls as a way of nurturing self-esteem and resilience. GirlVentures.org

OUTWARD BOUND: Outward Bound provides leadership training and wilderness adventure experiences to girls and boys ages 12 and up in locations throughout the world. OutwardBound.org

SHEJUMPS: SheJumps offers classes, workshops, and hands-on outdoor-skills training to girls and women of all ages and connects women and girls through community events. SheJumps.org

WOMEN'S WILDERNESS: Women's Wilderness has classes, outings, girls-only outdoor programs, camps, and after-school programs for girls of all ages interested in the outdoors. WomensWilderness.org

YWCA: At more than 160 years old, YWCA is one of the oldest women's organizations in the United States, and with three hundred local associations, it's also one of the most widespread. It offers outdoor-based summer camps and outings, in addition to courses and essential skills training like first aid and water safety, to girls of all ages. YWCA.org

> **TRY THIS!** Spend a day with a friend's troop or group. Find out what kinds of things they do, and meet some of the other members to see if it's right for you.

GAMES

. . . .

Being the keeper of a trove of games makes you a useful
and fun addition to any camp group. Learn the rules for
several types of games, so that you are always ready to help
organize the fun. Remember that getting outside can come
with long car rides or rainy days at camp, so bring games
for the car and tent too (see Assemble a Car-Camping
Activity Bin, page 72)! Your game stash could include:

- Deck of cards

- Mancala board

- Notepad and pen or pencil

- Frisbee

- Balls

Breaking the Ice

Icebreakers are games we play with new groups to get to
know one another. Great icebreakers tell us something
about one another or help us learn each other's names.
For groups with just a few new people and lots of familiar faces, try to make everyone at ease by playing a game
where everyone takes a turn like I spy and charades.

THE NAME GAME

For groups where everyone is new, play the name game.

WHAT YOU'LL NEED: A group of people (more than five works best)

GOAL: To learn each other's names

HOW TO PLAY: Gather in a circle, and have one person start by saying their name and something they like (favorite dessert, book, animal). The next person repeats the name and favorite thing of the person (or people) in front of them, then adds their own. The last person has the hardest job—they have to remember everyone!

Games for Two (or More)

Two-person games are perfect for rainy days in tents and long drives when space and people might be limited, and they can also be expanded to include a larger group. Here's a list of classics.

MEMORY

WHAT YOU'LL NEED: A deck of cards

GOAL: To collect the most pairs

HOW TO PLAY: Lay out all the cards facedown. Taking turns, turn two cards faceup. If they match (two jacks, for example), they are yours to take; if they don't match, turn them back over in place, and it's the next person's turn to try to remember where the matched pairs are. You can make this more difficult by adding a rule that matched pairs should be of the same color. Turn this into a craft project by creating your own set of memory cards based on nature. You can draw them or use rubber stamps, magazine clippings, or even pressed flowers to make your own unique pairs of cards.

MANCALA

WHAT YOU'LL NEED: A mancala board and stones (see Make Your Own Mancala Board, page 28, if you don't have these)

GOAL: To collect the most stones

HOW TO PLAY: Place four stones in each of your six pits (yours are the ones closest to you). The first player chooses a pit from their side and takes all the stones from it, moving around the board counterclockwise, placing one stone in each pit, and depositing a stone if they pass their own "store" (your store is where you keep your extra stones and is located at the ends of the board). If their last stone lands in an empty pit on their own side, they capture that stone and all the stones in the opposite pit for their store. You never need to place a stone in your opponent's store. If the last stone in your hand lands in your store, you get an extra turn. The game ends when one player has no more stones in their pits. The player with remaining stones gets to capture and store those stones. The player with the most stones in their store wins.

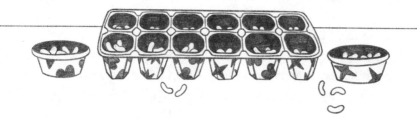

Make Your Own Mancala Board

Mancala is actually a group of games based on the moving of stones around a board; it began in Africa around 500 AD. The term "mancala" is derived from the Arabic word *naqala*, which means "to move." Like original mancala games, this version has you collect your own game pieces from the natural world.

WHAT YOU'LL NEED:
Sturdy cardboard egg carton
Scissors
Acrylic paint or markers
2 small cans (cat food, tuna, etc.)
Construction paper
Glue
48 small stones, shells, pinecones, dried berries or peas, or nuts

WHAT TO DO:

1. Cut the top off the egg carton. Decorate the carton with paint or markers, making sure one row of six is decorated differently from the other.

2. Clean and dry both cans. Measure and cut out two strips of construction paper that can wrap around the cans.

3. Glue the paper strips to the cans, and decorate each to match one side of the board. These are your stores.

4. Collect your game pieces. Since the color and shape of the pieces doesn't need to match, you can collect as many different kinds of pieces as you like, as long as they fit in your board. Look for dime- to nickel-sized shells, stones, or nuts whenever you're outside to make your game unique.

DID YOU KNOW? There are more card combinations in a deck of playing cards than there are stars in the Milky Way galaxy. That's more than four hundred billion!

WAR

WHAT YOU'LL NEED: A deck of cards

GOAL: To collect all the cards

HOW TO PLAY: Deal all the cards facedown, giving half the deck to each player. Both players turn one card faceup in the center at the same time. The player with the higher card takes both cards (aces are high) and moves them to the bottom of their hand. If the same card is thrown by both players—for instance, two queens—a war is started. Each player places one card facedown, then one card faceup. The person with the higher faceup card takes all four cards from the center. If there is still a tie, repeat the process using two facedown cards for a double war.

MORE GAMES FOR (AT LEAST) TWO

- Obstacle-course races (see page 47)
- Frisbee/catch
- Hopscotch
- I spy
- Chess and checkers (see page 72)
- Horseshoes/target toss
- Trail Tall Tales (see page 38)

Games for Four or More

CAPTURE THE FLAG

WHAT YOU'LL NEED: Something to serve as a flag for each team (a bandana, T-shirt, etc.). Whatever you use should be brightly colored, and each team's flag should be different from the other team's.

GOAL: To capture the other team's flag and return it to your territory

HOW TO PLAY: Choose teams, territories, and areas to be jails. Each team places its flag on its own territory, someplace visible and within reach of the smallest player. Teams cross into each other's territory to find and capture the flag. Players tagged while in enemy territory go to jail until they are rescued by being safely escorted to their home territory by a teammate.

KICK THE CAN

WHAT YOU'LL NEED: A soup or coffee can

GOAL: To be the last free player

HOW TO PLAY: Place the can in a central location, and choose an area to be the jail, a person to be the kicker, and a person to be "it." All the "not its" hide after their chosen kicker kicks the can. The "it" chases after and searches for players as soon as the can is kicked. Tagged players go straight to jail, but if they spot a hidden player, they call out that player's name and hiding place. The hidden player then must run to and kick the can before being tagged and sent to jail. The last free player wins and becomes the next "it."

I DOUBT IT

WHAT YOU'LL NEED: A deck of cards

GOAL: To be the first to get rid of all your cards

HOW TO PLAY: Deal all the cards between each player; it's okay if the piles are uneven. The first player has to play aces, even if they don't have any. They lay a card or several cards facedown in the middle and announce how many (for example, "two aces"). If everyone believes them, the cards remain in the center, and the next player continues with twos, the next with threes, and so on. If someone calls out, "I doubt it," the cards are checked. If the last player was lying, they take back their cards and any underlying cards. If they were telling the truth, their accuser takes the pile.

MORE GREAT GAMES FOR FOUR OR MORE

- Relay races
- Freeze tag
- Charades
- Red rover

- Red light, green light
- Hide-and-seek
- Scavenger hunt (see page 82)

INCLUDING EVERYONE

Being a part of a team or troop means working and playing with lots of different kinds of people. Sometimes getting along with others or feeling accepted can be really challenging. Maybe you're new to the group, or the troop leader plays favorites, or you did something embarrassing just once and everyone still thinks it's funny; people don't get along for all sorts of reasons. Sometimes people can just be mean. The most common reason those people lash out at others is because they secretly feel badly about themselves.

Do not take bad things other people say to or about you to heart.

So, you probably won't become best friends with everyone. It's still important to treat everyone with respect, so that you can work together toward your common goals. Remember, different types of personalities, cultures, and ideas are useful in a group, since there are always lots of different kinds of tasks and challenges. The more different kinds of people in your group, the more ideas, skills, and helping hands you have. Part of being in a group is making sure that you practice kindness and acceptance and stand up to bullies. Do that, and you'll always make some friends.

Tips for Getting Along in Groups

- Choose games and activities that everyone can participate in.

- Play by fair rules that you agree on *before* you begin.

- Change leaders and roles frequently, giving everyone a chance to be in charge, go first, and try each task.

- Divide tasks, let everyone do part of the work, and expect everyone to help out.

- Bring extra and come prepared to share what you have with others.

- Stay positive! Take setbacks as challenges, offer solutions rather than complaints, and be ready with a smile, compliment, or pep talk.

TRY THIS! Get a new perspective. Pair with a friend to experience your surroundings with a blindfold or earplugs. Take turns acting as each other's guide. What are the challenges and advantages? How do you have to change and adapt to get things done? What new things do you notice when you rely on other senses?

Invent Your Own Game

Many of the games we play today, like kick the can and hide-and-seek, started out as street games invented and played by kids who lived in the city. They used the things around them, like discarded cans, sticks, or the nooks and crannies of their own street, to inspire them. Use your favorite outdoor place to inspire a new game that's all your own. Maybe you'll invent a new kind of tag using rocks and trees from your campsite as bases or design a new "seek and discover" game that's inspired by local critters.

**WHAT YOU *MIGHT* NEED
(IT'S ALL UP TO YOU!):**
Paper and pencil
Balls
Flags
Timers
Sidewalk chalk
Imagination!

WHAT TO DO:

1. Choose what kind of game you want to play: relay, observation, team game, etc.

2. Choose what the action or goal of the game is: finding, chasing, tagging, collecting.

3. Decide if there are points, time-outs, or other special rules, and write them down.

4. Mark the boundaries or bases with flags or sidewalk chalk or by using landmarks.

5. If you have teams, decide how they will be chosen: by captains, by counting off, etc.

6. Decide how turns will be taken and how the game starts and ends.

7. Gather any needed equipment.

8. Teach your new game to a group of friends or family.

JULIETTE GORDON LOW
Founder of the Girl Scouts

Juliette Gordon Low was born in Savannah, Georgia, in 1860 and was known for her adventurous spirit and ability to overcome obstacles (she lost nearly all her hearing by the time she was twenty). She was an early champion of the idea that young women should be encouraged to travel, adventure, and learn new skills. After being introduced to the Boy Scouts movement while in Europe in 1912, she returned to Georgia to start a small troop of girls from a variety of cultural and economic backgrounds, insisting that "Girl Scouting and Girl Guiding can be the magic thread which links the youth of the world together." That troop would become the Girl Scouts, which now has close to two million members worldwide!

TRAIL TALL TALES

· ·

For each updated fairy tale, read just the descriptions
for each word in parentheses out loud, and ask a friend to
think up the missing words, writing them on a separate
piece of paper or a photocopy of this page. When all the
words have been chosen, read your hilarious story out loud.
Take turns switching roles to see how the story changes!

Reminder:

NOUN: a person, place, or thing

PLURAL: more than one

VERB: action word

ADJECTIVE: describes a noun

(Boy's Name) *and Gretel*

One afternoon **(Same boy's name)** and Gretel took a walk in
the woods, carefully leaving a trail of **(food, plural)** behind
them to mark their way. But when they tried to return
on their path, they discovered that it had been eaten by
(type of animal, plural). As they wandered farther into the
woods, they found a magical cottage made entirely out of
(type of food) and candied **(type of flower, plural)**, with a
big sign reading "No Eating." After such a long day, **(Same
boy's name)** was hungry and **(emotion)** and wanted to try
a few bites of the house. Gretel, though, knew that those
flowers would make him turn **(color)** and **(verb)**, so she
stopped him just in time. Instead, she gathered wood for a
fire to keep them warm until night fell and used the night
sky to find their way home.

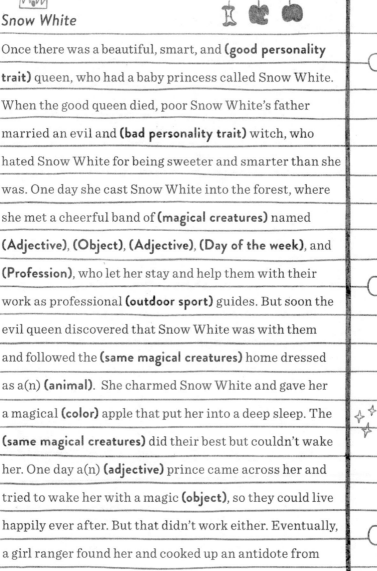

Snow White

Once there was a beautiful, smart, and **(good personality trait)** queen, who had a baby princess called Snow White. When the good queen died, poor Snow White's father married an evil and **(bad personality trait)** witch, who hated Snow White for being sweeter and smarter than she was. One day she cast Snow White into the forest, where she met a cheerful band of **(magical creatures)** named **(Adjective)**, **(Object)**, **(Adjective)**, **(Day of the week)**, and **(Profession)**, who let her stay and help them with their work as professional **(outdoor sport)** guides. But soon the evil queen discovered that Snow White was with them and followed the **(same magical creatures)** home dressed as a(n) **(animal)**. She charmed Snow White and gave her a magical **(color)** apple that put her into a deep sleep. The **(same magical creatures)** did their best but couldn't wake her. One day a(n) **(adjective)** prince came across her and tried to wake her with a magic **(object)**, so they could live happily ever after. But that didn't work either. Eventually, a girl ranger found her and cooked up an antidote from

(plant) leaves and **(type of food, plural)**. She and Snow White became good friends and, with the **(same magical creatures)**, started their own wilderness rescue unit.

(Color)-i-locks

There once was a family of three **(animals)**: Mama, Papa, and the Wee One. One morning, while camping in (place), they sat down to a breakfast of **(type of food)**, but it was too hot, so they decided to go for a(n) **(outdoor activity)** while it cooled. Along came **(Same color)-i-locks**, who had been out **(different outdoor activity, ending in "ing")**. She was so hungry she couldn't resist tasting some of their delicious food. First, she tried the big bowl, but it was too **(adjective)**; then she tried the medium bowl, but it was too **(adjective)**. The littlest bowl was just right, so she ate it all up. Next, she looked for a place to **(verb)**. She tried the **(adjective)** tent first, but it was too **(same adjective)**. Then she tried the **(adjective)** tent, but it was too **(same adjective)**. But the last tent was just right. While **(Same color)**-i-locks was **(same verb, ending in "ing")**, the animals got home. Papa looked around and hollered, "**(Exclamation)**!" Someone had been eating his breakfast! Someone had eaten Mama's and Wee One's too! Then they checked their tents and found **(Same color)**-i-locks asleep! They **(type of noise, ending in "ed")** as loud as they could and chased her with **(type of camp gear, plural)**, but that didn't scare **(Same color)**-i-locks, who ran around **(type of action, ending in "ing")**, returning their camp to the way she found it, taking only a picture to remind her of her encounter.

CHAPTER 3

OUTDOOR PURSUITS

On the loose to climb a mountain,
On the loose where I am free.

—CAMP SONG

There's a lot more to do outside than camping and hiking
(although those are fun too). There's loads of exciting,
interesting, and quirky outdoor sports and hobbies. These
activities usually require some special equipment and
skills, and some kinds of sports are better suited for some
places than others (Florida might be a great place to learn
to surf, but not to ski!). Remember, it's always best to try
new things with someone more experienced than you and
to wear your safety equipment!

LAND SPORTS

BOULDERING: Bouldering is a kind of rock climbing that doesn't use ropes, anchors, or harnesses, so it's a great way to get into climbing without spending a lot of money on gear or taking on big heights right away. This is a great outdoor sport because you can keep practicing all year long at climbing gyms, on playgrounds, and at parks with practice walls.

HORSEBACK RIDING: Horseback riding lets you travel long distances in the outdoors. It is also one of the oldest forms of human transportation! You can try out riding for an hour, a day, or even longer if you find a camp, guided tour, or equestrian center near you.

MOUNTAIN BIKING: Mountain biking takes the sport of cycling off road and onto the trails. You can start using any bike you have on easy trails before investing in a mountain bike. And you can always practice at home: every time you ride your bike, experiment with riding on different kinds of surfaces, like grass and gravel.

SANDBOARDING: Sandboarding is exactly what it sounds like—sliding down massive sand dunes on a board like snowboarding or skateboarding! Sandboarding started in ancient Egypt, where people used wooden boards to slide across the sand. Now it's a worldwide, competitive sport! You can start by practicing on small dunes using an old disc sled or a piece of cardboard.

SPELUNKING: "Spelunking" is the name for exploring caves. Spelunkers use different skills, like rock climbing, hiking, and scuba diving, to explore vast networks of caves. Urban spelunking—exploring old, worn-out, and underground parts of cities—has become a popular way to get started, and to get used to the dark!

OTHER LAND SPORTS:

- Backpacking
- Hiking
- Mountaineering
- Rock climbing

DID YOU KNOW? Caves are made when water dissolves rock as it makes its way down *joints* (cracks in rocks). It can take millions of years for caves to form.

Make a Mini Obstacle-Course Trail

Want the fun and challenge of outdoor sports closer to home? You can practice skills and compete with your friends on your own mini course that you design. Harder courses combine several modes of travel (like running, biking, and climbing); include obstacles, challenges, or checkpoints; and take an interesting path. You can make your course as simple or complex as you want. Some fun challenges to include are:

- Mud puddles and gravel patches
- Trails and switchbacks (zigzags)
- Over-and-under obstacles
- Around-and-through obstacles
- Balance beam or follow-the-line challenges (hop, skip, or cartwheel along a marked path)
- Challenge stations (stop and balance on one foot for 30 seconds, build a rock cairn, etc.)
- Wading pools for "water sports"
- Play equipment for climbing challenges
- Different ways of moving on foot (run, walk, hop, skip, crawl, etc.)

CONTINUED

WHAT YOU'LL NEED:
Scratch paper
Pencil
Mode(s) of travel: skateboard, skates, bike
Water: sprinkler, garden hose, plastic bin, and/or wading pool
Land surfaces: grass, pavement, gravel, dirt, sand, and/or bark dust
Route and station markers: chalk, bins, flags, chairs, cones, sticks, and/or ribbons
Obstacles: tables, chairs, trash cans, tents, trees, shrubs, and/or rocks
Construction or scratch paper
Markers
Stopwatch or kitchen timer
Safety gear: helmet, shoes, pads, etc.

WHAT TO DO:

1. Ask permission and get help from an adult to choose a safe place for your course, especially if you want to use shared areas like sidewalks or neighbors' yards.

2. Choose your mode (or modes) of transportation. Will you walk, run, bike, or climb? Or some combination?

3. Plan your route. Choose a path that will take more than two minutes to get through. Think about whether your course will be a circle or an out and back. Make sure you pick a route that has low traffic. A challenging course will have more than one kind of surface, so look for concrete, grass, and a great place to put a mud puddle and sand or gravel trap.

4. Choose your obstacles and challenges. Try to find at least one obstacle to circle, one to weave through, and one place to duck. Other ideas are balance, run, walk, hop, ride, splash, climb, and toss.

5. Build your course, marking it with route and station markers. Use your sidewalk chalk to mark pathways on sidewalks and driveways. Do they zigzag or squiggle? You get to choose the route.

6. Make a sign with instructions for each station along the route. Use easy-to-see colors.

7. Make a test run, and decide what can be improved.

8. Run time trials! You can time yourself, time your friends while taking turns, or have a free-for-all where every-one starts at the same time and competes to finish the course first!

WATER SPORTS

· ·

> **TRY THIS!** See how long you can hold your breath. Is it easier in cold water? It should be. Humans have a natural response to cold water that slows down body functions, making us need less oxygen. The world record for breath holding is more than 22 minutes!

FISHING: Fishing has always been an important survival skill for humans, but it's also a challenging outdoor sport. There are even national championships! The easiest way to start is to use a fish trap (see Build Your Own Fish Trap Viewer, page 52), jar, or net to see what kinds of small creatures and critters you can catch before moving on to a rod and reel.

PADDLEBOARDING: In paddleboarding, you stand or kneel on a large board and paddle across relatively calm water, like a lake. It's a good beginning water sport because it combines the paddling skills needed for kayaking and canoeing with the board skills you need for sports like surfing and windsurfing.

> **DID YOU KNOW?** Canoes used to be carved out of trees or made from strips of bark. The oldest-known canoes were found in the Netherlands and are thought to be nearly 9,000 years old!

SCUBA DIVING/SNORKELING: Scuba diving and snorkeling let you explore the world beneath the water and are sports you can practice all year at your local swimming pool. To get started, use goggles to swim underwater, then practice breathing with a snorkel, and add in your diving and flipper skills by chasing weighted water rings or other objects that will sink. Once you've mastered snorkeling, you can train to become a scuba diver (which requires a special certification) and carry your own oxygen with you to explore greater depths.

SWIMMING: Being a strong swimmer is the most important part of being able to do any water-based activity. You can find swim classes at local community centers and pools, through summer programs, and sometimes even through your own school. Make sure you get swim tested at a local pool every year, so that you know what level you are, and *always* wear a life vest or personal flotation device when you are on any kind of boat.

WHITE-WATER RAFTING: White-water rafting is an exciting group sport that is easy to participate in for a day trip or longer, if you go with a tour or an experienced guide. White-water rafts are designed for navigating rivers, especially the rapids formed by water flowing over rocks and small falls, which makes every river run an adventure.

OTHER WATER SPORTS:

- Kayaking/canoeing
- Sailing
- Surfing
- Waterskiing
- Windsurfing

Build Your Own Fish Trap Viewer

There's a lot of life to see in even the smallest of streams, if everything would just stop moving around so fast! One way to get to see what's living in the water is to scoop it all up into a fish viewer—a fish trap designed to let you capture and release small critters.

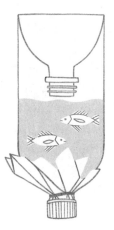

WHAT YOU'LL NEED:
Box cutter
2 (2-liter) bottles
Ruler
Rubber cement or hot glue
Scissors
Cheesecloth
Rubber band
Twine/nylon cord
Duct tape

WHAT TO DO:

1. Cut the top off one of the 2-liter bottles about 4 inches down from the top. Discard the cap and bottom half.

2. Cut the bottom off the second bottle about 4 inches up from the base. Keep the cap but discard the bottom.

3. Run glue along the bottom of the first bottle, and nest it in the second bottle.

4. Run glue around the connection of the two bottles to seal them together, and hold in place for 2 minutes. Set aside until dry, for at least 10 minutes.

5. Cut an approximately 3-inch square of cheesecloth (you may fold it over to double the thickness) and secure it over the mouth of the trap with the rubber band.

6. Tie two loops of twine around the trap, about one-quarter of the way in from each end, making a handle.

7. Secure the handle with a thin strip of duct tape.

8. Submerge the trap in water, allowing it to flow through the cheesecloth. When you catch a fish, secure the bottle cap back over the bottle, so you can lift your viewer out of the water without all the water draining out.

9. To return your fish to the stream, place the trap back in the water before removing the bottle cap and cheesecloth and letting it swim away.

SNOW SPORTS

· ·

CROSS-COUNTRY SKIING: Cross-country skiing combines the fun of downhill skiing with the challenge of longer distances (and some serious stamina-building uphills). The challenge of learning this skill is worth it—cross-country skis are one of the fastest ways to travel in the outdoors in winter.

> **TRY THIS!** Find a demo day at an outdoor retailer or club near you. Check the websites of your local gear shops and outdoor groups for a training event that is open to the public. It's a fun way to try a sport for a day!

DOGSLEDDING: Dogsledding, sometimes called "mushing," is another sport based on an old form of transportation. In dogsledding, a team of trained dogs pulls you and your sled across the snow and ice. It takes many years to train a team of dogs, but you can try dogsledding for a day trip or longer in many places that are cold most of the year, like Alaska or Canada.

MOUNTAIN CLIMBING: Mountain climbing, or mountaineering, refers to climbing to the top of very high mountains. Mountaineers use a combination of hiking, rock and ice climbing, and navigation skills to reach a summit. You can start training for mountain climbing by summiting smaller hills and peaks in your area.

DID YOU KNOW? The tallest mountain in the world is actually an island. Mauna Kea, in Hawai'i, reaches only 13,796 feet above sea level, but it stretches another 19,700 feet below the surface of the water to the ocean floor. All told, it stands nearly a mile higher than Mount Everest!

OTHER SNOW SPORTS:

- Downhill skiing/snowboarding
- Ice skating/hockey
- Sledding/luge
- Snowshoeing

LIBBY RIDDLES
Dogsledding Champion

Libby Riddles was 28 when she became the first woman to win the Iditarod, the world's most competitive and challenging dogsledding race. The Iditarod crosses about 1,000 miles of mountains, ice fields, and tundra in Alaska and is considered one of the hardest races on earth. It's so hard, in fact, that they even give a prize (the red lantern) to last place! Libby's win, in 1985, was especially exciting because she was the only racer brave enough to set out into blizzard conditions, and it paid off! Now, Libby helps others realize their dogsledding dreams by raising dog teams and working as a guide. She has also received humanitarian awards for best treatment of competition dogs!

OTHER OUTDOOR ACTIVITIES

GEOCACHING AND ORIENTEERING: Geocaching uses GPS coordinates (latitude and longitude) to guide searchers to waypoints and hidden treasures. Orienteering is the sport of *navigation*: getting from one place to another with a map and compass. Learn how to use maps and navigate in Chapter 8: Maps and Weather (page 159).

ROCKHOUNDING: "Rockhounding" is what rock, mineral, and geology enthusiasts call the hunt for rock specimens. Rock hounds dig, scrape, and pan for samples, often then cutting and polishing them into museum-quality specimens.

STARGAZING AND ASTRONOMY: Astronomy is the science of the skies. Astronomers use telescopes, high-resolution cameras, and other astral equipment for a chance to see a comet, meteor shower, or eclipses.

TRACKING AND BIRDING: Tracking and birding are outdoor activities focused entirely on finding and observing wildlife. In tracking you use footprints and other signs of life (see Chapter 10: Things to Look For, page 223) to find and follow animals.

TREE CLIMBING: Recreational tree climbing takes the equipment and skills of rock climbing and timber harvesting and uses them to explore the forest canopy.

DEER
TRACK

HARE
TRACK

FOX
TRACK

Pan for Gold (and Other Metals)

Panning is a very old method of mining by hand that uses water to sort and separate gold and other precious stones from dirt, sand, and sediment. Miners and prospectors still use panning today in the hopes of striking it rich! Once you get the hang of panning, you can start bagging and tagging your finds with the help of a geology or panning field guide. There are lots of semiprecious stones and metals that can be found using this technique. See Chapter 10: Things to Look For (page 223) for information on how to make observations of rock and sediment.

WHAT YOU'LL NEED:

Panning pan, metal pie pan, or large plastic Frisbee
Kitchen sieve or sifter
Magnet
Plastic bags (for samples)
Markers

WHAT TO DO:

1. Choose a location with lots of loose sediment (sand, silt, and gravel) at the edges of shallow water, like streams, ocean shores, or lakesides.

2. Scoop one or two handfuls of sediment into your pan, and submerge it into the water. Shift the pan gently up and down, letting the lighter bits float away (gold and other metals are dense and will sink to the bottom of the pan).

3. Lift the pan out of the water and gently swirl the remaining sediment and water in a circle, allowing the medium-sized particles to wash out. Repeat this process, adding more water, until most of the sediment is removed. This step is great for finding agates and other interesting nonmetallic stones.

4. Sort the remaining sediment by size using a kitchen sieve or sifter, and separate out iron-bearing minerals, like magnetite, using a magnet. Look in the remaining sediment for fragments and flakes with a shiny, metallic luster—they might be gold!

5. Place your sorted material in a plastic bag. Label it with the date, location, and what kind of rock you think it is.

PART 2

the basics

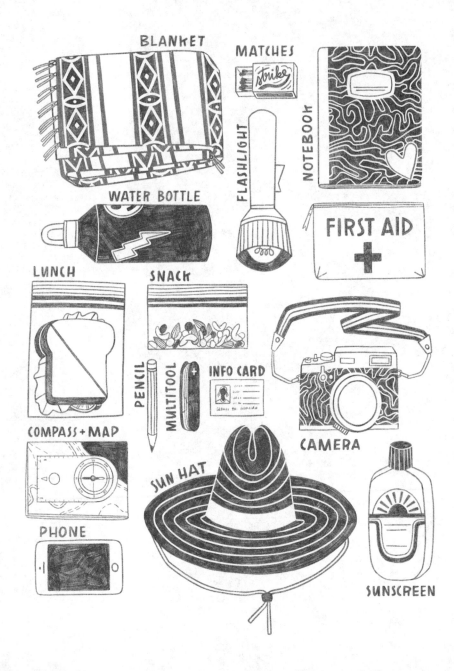

CHAPTER 4

WHAT TO BRING

Black socks, the longer you wear them the blacker they get.

—CAMP SONG

Outside, you need to be able to carry, pull, or load everything you bring to your site by yourself or with the help of your group. For that reason, try to bring only the things you really need. A good way to pack is to make two lists, one of things you *have* to have (like water), the other of things you *want* to have (like a book). Gather and pack all the things you need first, then lift up your bag and feel how heavy it is. *Then* choose which things to bring with you from your list of wants. It's never a good idea to travel with something you can't stand to lose, so leave your most special treasures at home.

PACKING

It can seem like a whole lot to get organized when packing, but the good news is, once you've done it the first time, it gets easier every time. Use a list, like the ones here, so you won't forget something important.

What to Bring for Just a Day

You should be able to carry all of your gear for just a day in a backpack or fanny pack. It's important that you are comfortable and able to use your hands, so test it out before you go.

- Water
- Guidebook, map, and compass
- Lunch and snacks
- First-aid kit (see Chapter 9: Surprises and Mishaps, page 193)
- Blanket
- Cell phone
- Sunscreen and sunglasses
- Hat (sun hat or beanie, depending on the season)
- Multitool or pocketknife
- Waterproof matches
- Flashlight
- Emergency and medical information card

OPTIONAL EXTRAS:

- Camera
- Binoculars
- Field guide

- Swimsuit and towel
- Notebook and pencil
- Bandana

GREAT WAYS TO USE A BANDANA:

- Neck cooler
- Headband
- Packing pouch
- Pot holder

- Bandage
- Sling
- Washcloth

PACKING POUCH

NECK COOLER

BANDAGE

NOTE ON FIELD JOURNALS

Many of the activities and projects described in the following chapters use a field journal (or log), a special notebook that people use for writing, drawing, and recording the things they see and do outside, a lot like an outdoor diary. Take a moment now to find your own field journal to use as you read and on your adventures. You can use any blank notebook or a specially designed field journal with space for different kinds of observations.

What to Bring for Overnight Camping

If you are staying one or more nights at the same cabin or campground, you can (and need to) bring more stuff. Before you start throwing in everything and the kitchen sink, make sure you have all the essentials—especially toilet paper!

- Tent with rain fly, ground tarp, and extra stakes
- Bedding, pillows, and sleeping pads
- Camp stove and fuel
- Cooking utensils and dishware (plates, cups, bowls, etc.)
- Food and beverage coolers with ice
- Camp table and chairs
- Large lanterns and/or flashlights

- Water jugs
- Sun/rain protection: tarps, pop-up canopies, or umbrellas
- Towels
- Toilet paper
- Bathroom essentials
- Clothing (see What to Wear, page 75)
- Small ax and shovel
- First-aid kit (see Chapter 9: Surprises and Mishaps, page 193)
- Rope and/or twine
- Garbage bags
- Day-trip pack and gear

TIP: Keep a small pack of baby wipes in your pack or pocket—you can use them as toilet paper or to clean your hands. Remember to bring an extra ziplock bag to pack them out in!

What to Bring for Longer Tours

You need all of the same basic things for longer trips as you do for any kind of overnight camping, but be prepared to wear things more than once. You will also want to look for versions of tents, sleeping bags, stoves, and lights that are designed to be smaller and lighter, so you can carry them with you more easily. If you are in a group, everyone should be responsible for their own water, clothing, bedding, first aid, and personal items. The rest of the equipment and food should be divided between packs, boats, or saddlebags (however you are stowing and transporting your gear), so that everyone shares the load. You'll know you've brought too much if you can't fit it all into your bags.

HOW TO PACK YOUR BACKPACKING BACKPACK

1. Place your sleeping bag at the bottom of your pack to keep it clean and dry.

2. Load heavier gear like tents, food, and pots and pans in the middle.

3. Fill the top with lighter gear, like clothing.

4. Place things you may need on the trail, like water and your first-aid kit, in the outside pockets.

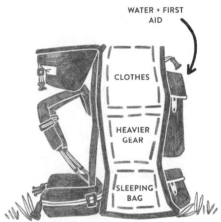

5. Try on your pack and walk around for a few minutes to make sure it's comfortable and most of the weight sits on your hips. If not, adjust the straps. If this is your first time using this pack, try a short walk around your neighborhood or in a nearby park before setting off for a longer trip.

IS YOUR PACK TOO HEAVY? Most kids can carry 10 to 20 pounds in a day pack and 30 to 40 pounds in a backpacking pack, but this varies a lot based on height and age, so see what works for you.

Can I Bring My Phone?

You can. In fact, you should. Phones are actually an important piece of your gear. They can be everything from journals to flashlights, compasses, mirrors, and cameras and are especially useful if you're packing light—you can load them up with your favorite books without making your pack heavier! There are also field-guide apps that will show you the constellations, let you look up the name of a bird by its call, or help you identify a plant. Download apps that suit your interests before you head out, and make sure they will work without Wi-Fi or cell service. Most importantly, you'll need your phone in an emergency, even if you have to get back to the car to get a signal. But be careful not to use them for music or playing anything with the sound on. Most animals can hear far better than we can, so they can tell when we are coming. Even fish can hear you from the banks!

DID YOU KNOW? Moths have the most sensitive hearing of all animals. Their ears pick up even the super-high-frequency sounds of their primary predators—bats.

FIVE GREAT WAYS TO USE YOUR PHONE OUTSIDE:

- Magnifying glass
- Camera
- Compass
- Distance tracker
- Flashlight

Assemble a Car-Camping Activity Bin

Once you get to your camp, you'll have a lot of time for playing and having fun. Make sure you never get bored by assembling your own camp activity bin that comes with you whenever you go car camping and even has its own game board. Below are some suggestions to get you started. What else can you think of to add to your bin?

**WHAT YOU'LL NEED
FOR INSIDE THE BIN:**
Deck of cards
Yarn and/or cord
Dice
Frisbee and/or panning pan
Paper and colored pencils
  (don't forget a sharpener!)
  or crayons
Fish trap or water viewer (see
  Build Your Own Fish Trap
  Viewer, page 52)
Sports gear (like helmets, bike
  pumps, goggles, ball pumps,
  and balls)
Collection boxes, nets, and
  flower presses

**WHAT YOU'LL NEED
FOR THE BIN:**
Large plastic tote
Pencil
Ruler
Permanent markers
Construction paper
Scissors
Hot glue or rubber cement
24 bottle caps

WHAT TO DO:

1. Gather the contents of your bin. The goal is to keep
   your bin packed and ready to go at any time, so try to
   pack things you don't use every day. If you do bring an
   item you use frequently (like your favorite Frisbee),
   either try to remember to unpack it right away when
   you get home, or decide that the bin is its new home
   and always store it there.

2. On the box lid, draw a square that measures 2 by 2 inches.
   Using this first square as a guide, mark with a pencil eight
   (2-inch) ticks on each side of the square. Connect the
   marks with lines to form a grid, and draw over them with
   permanent marker. You should end up with a grid of eight

CONTINUED

squares by eight squares—sixty-four squares in all! Starting with the upper-right-hand corner, color in every other square a dark color. This is your game board.

3. On a piece of construction paper, trace twelve circles using your bottle caps. Choose a different color paper and repeat. Cut out the circles and attach them to your bottle caps using hot glue or rubber cement. These are your checkers pieces. If you want chess pieces, repeat this process, then use your markers to draw pictures of the chess pieces on each piece. (Need the rules for checkers or chess? Try a Hoyle's or Klutz book of games.)

4. On the inside of the box lid, make a list of the bin's contents.

5. On one end of the box, make a list of all your favorite games to play outside (see Chapter 2: Groups, Troops, and Sisterhoods, page 21).

6. On the other side of the box, make two outdoor-themed scavenger lists (see page 82 for a sample list).

7. Pack your bin and decorate the two remaining sides with drawings of your favorite animals, plants, or constellations (see Chapter 10: Things to Look For, page 223).

WHAT TO WEAR

Clothing keeps you warm in cold weather or cool in hot weather and protects your arms and legs from bites, scratches, and sunburns. Some outdoor activities have special clothing that helps keep you safe or lets you move more easily, but most of the time, you'll be able to wear clothing that you already own.

Tips for outdoor clothing:

- Always bring one layer of clothing more than you think you will need; so, even if it's a sunny day, you should bring a warm top layer, like a coat, with you. Remember, the weather can change quickly.

- Wear a skirt. Skirts and dresses are great to wear outside (with a pair of shorts underneath)—they keep you cool and make it easy to change.

- Or wear pants! Pants protect your legs better than anything else.

- Put something on your head. Whether it's to block the sun or keep your body heat from escaping, you'll be glad you did.

- Choose clothes that can get dirty. Some of the fun of being outside is the opportunity to get dirty, so bring clothes you don't mind running around and being scruffy in.

- Wear clothing that is comfortable and gives you a full range of motion. Outside is not the place for skinny jeans so tight you can't bend your knees.
- Be yourself! Wear colors and styles that make you feel good about yourself.

DID YOU KNOW? Temperatures in the desert can differ by more than 50 degrees Fahrenheit in a single day! That means you could need shorts and a T-shirt in the afternoon and a heavy winter coat at night!

Clothing packing list:

- Undershirt or sports bra and underwear
- Tank tops
- Long underwear tops and bottoms
- Short- and long-sleeved tops or dresses
- Sweater, fleece layer, and/or vest
- Pants, shorts, and/or skirts
- Socks
- Topcoat (fleece or down coat)
- Beanie
- Gloves or mittens
- Windbreaker
- Rain and/or sun hat
- Rain jacket and pants or poncho
- Don't forget your swimsuit!!

TRY THIS! Make your own rain poncho out of a large garbage bag by cutting holes for your head and arms. Reinforce the side seams and add some flair with your favorite funky-patterned duct tape. Keep it in your day pack for unexpected showers.

Clothing for Winter Weather

Choosing the right layers is extra important in winter weather. Some fabrics are better at holding in the heat than others, especially if they get wet. The warmest and safest fabrics and materials for winter weather come from nature, like down and wool, or are synthetics made especially for the outdoors. The worst fabric to choose is cotton, which actually pulls the heat from your body when wet.

Winter weather clothing list:

- Long underwear tops and bottoms
- Insulated gloves or mittens
- Rain pants and jacket
- Fleece, down vest and/ or jacket
- Snow pants
- Beanie
- Hiking or insulated socks
- Water-resistant hiking boots or snow boots

ANIMAL EXPERTS AT STAYING WARM

Humans have always taken a cue from other animals when it comes to dressing for winter weather. Here are just a few of the animal experts that inspire our outdoor clothing now.

BIRDS: Bird feathers are specially designed to capture the heat from a bird's body and hold it in the tiny air spaces between each piece of the feather. That's why down coats and blankets are so good at keeping us warm.

BIGHORN SHEEP: Tiny air pockets are what make wool so great for the outdoors also. Not only can it keep you warm even when it's wet; it's also fire resistant. Unlike feathers, wool is extra sturdy, making it a perfect outdoor fabric.

POLAR BEARS: Polar bears combine heat-trapping air pockets in their fur with black skin that soaks up and stores the sun's heat rays (called *radiation*). You can re-create this effect by wearing dark colors in the snow to absorb the sun and light colors on hot days.

WHAT TO PUT ON YOUR FEET

Always wear a sturdy pair of closed-toed shoes when you go outside. Avoid wearing a brand-new pair of shoes out hiking in case it takes a while to break them in—otherwise, you could end up with sore spots or blisters (see page 151). For longer trips on foot, you'll need a pair of hiking boots. Flip-flops are great to bring to wear around camp but aren't a good choice for most outdoor activities.

Sometimes, however, your feet will get wet. You'll forge across streams, have waves rush over your feet, and tromp through puddles. It's all part of the adventure! If your feet do get wet, try to change your socks and dry out your shoes as soon as possible. If you know that you're going to be near water or see that it's a rainy day, wear rain boots or your most waterproof pair of shoes.

DID YOU KNOW? Girls used to wear layers and layers of thick skirts and petticoats to keep warm, plus corsets and other purely decorative clothing that made it difficult (if not impossible) to move around. Imagine trying to climb a mountain in a hoopskirt!

LAURA INGALLS WILDER
Pioneer Girl

Laura Ingalls Wilder was born in a log cabin in Wisconsin in 1867 to a pioneer family that called her "half pint." In spite of her little nickname, she did big things. She spent her childhood living on the wild frontier lands of the American West, where she milked cows, made her own candles and butter, helped to harvest crops, and played outside most of the time. She became famous for writing about her life on the prairie and for her vivid descriptions of the land, plants and animals, and challenges of the American West. Her first book, *Little House in the Big Woods*, was published in 1932 and was followed by several other successful books about what life was like on the frontier and how her family overcame storms, dry seasons, locusts, illness, and more to build a new life. In fact, her books about life as a pioneer girl were so popular they inspired a television show, *Little House on the Prairie*, which ran for nearly ten years!

GIRL'S GUIDE SCAVENGER HUNT

Go outside and search for the following items. Once you find one, record it in your field journal. Remember, leave what you find where you found it, so that other creatures (and people!) can enjoy it.

- Something big
- Something small
- Something round
- Something shiny
- Something blue
- Something yellow
- A place where something lives
- Something smelly
- A footprint or animal track
- A living creature
- Two kinds of rocks
- Three kinds of plants
- One old thing
- One young thing
- Something you think is beautiful
- Something you think is interesting
- Two other things

CHAPTER 5

MAKING YOUR HOME AWAY FROM HOME

Home, home on the range,
Where the deer and the antelope play.

—DANIEL KELLEY AND BREWSTER HIGLEY

Camp is more than just a tent in the woods; it's your home away from home, so it's important to have everything you need to feel comfortable. Good campsites have all the parts of a home: warm beds, a kitchen, and an area where people can gather to talk, play, and relax. In this chapter, we'll talk about ways to make your campsite feel cozy.

DID YOU KNOW? *Hygge* (pronounced "HOO-gah") is the Danish concept of cozy, especially the kind of cozy that comes from a warm fire, good food, and the company of friends. The idea of *hygge* developed as a way to combat the cold and dark of a long winter.

CHOOSING A CAMPSITE

A lot of campsites are already laid out for you with a ready-made fire pit, picnic table, and level place to put your tent, but sometimes you'll be making camp without those things. In that case, you get to choose your site. The general rule of thumb is to look for a site that is relatively open and level—you don't want too many plants to get trampled or have a bunch of roots digging into your back all night.

Campsite checklist:

☐ 200 feet from any lake or stream (about one hundred big steps)

☐ 100 feet from the trail (about the length of a basketball court)

☐ Level ground for a tent

☐ Logs or rocks for seating and kitchen

☐ No overhead hazards (falling limbs or rocks)

Setting Up Camp

Once you have a site, you're ready to set up your camp:

1. Clear any large sticks or debris from the ground.

2. Pick out your tent site(s) and set up the tent(s).

3. Put kitchen items and coolers in the kitchen area.

4. Set out chairs and lanterns. Hang rain or shade tarps.

5. Set up your bedding and stow your gear inside the tent, putting aside a warm layer and your pajamas, as well as a flashlight, for easy access after dark.

6. Gather wood for your fire.

7. If needed, hang or secure your food away from animals (see Chapter 6: Good Grub, page 107).

Make your campsite more fun with some of these cool camp extras:

- Solar-powered path and string lights
- Oscillating/multicolored LED lanterns
- Telescopes
- Hammocks
- Gaming area for badminton, horseshoe, or croquet sets

Notice that a bathroom is not on the list of things in a campsite. That's because you should use the bathroom far from your campsite; that helps keep camp clean, keeps animals away, and gives everyone privacy (see Chapter 7: Girl Stuff, page 139, for more on camp bathrooms).

TRY THIS! Sleep out under the stars in just your sleeping bag for a night, without a tent or shelter (this is best done in the summer).

Tents

The most common way to sleep outside is in a tent. Tents come in all kinds of shapes and sizes. There are tiny tents that you can barely sit up in, big family tents with multiple rooms, and even hanging hammock tents. Most tents have three layers: the ground tarp, which keeps the bottom of the tent clean and dry; the tent and poles; and the rain fly, which keeps rain off the tent. Helping to set up the tent is a great way to make yourself useful at camp.

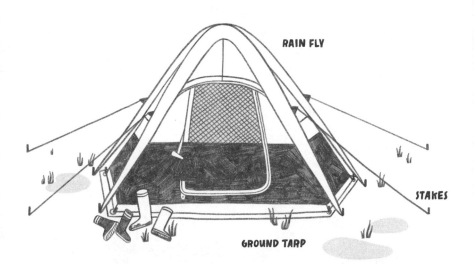

RAIN FLY

STAKES

GROUND TARP

How to pitch a tent:

1. Clear your tent site of all sticks, rocks, and other debris. Carefully pat down any live vegetation.

2. Place the ground tarp where you want your tent to be and stake it down.

3. Lay your tent out on the ground tarp and assemble your poles.

4. Run the poles through the hooks or sleeves, and secure the ends.

5. Stake down the tent using the anchor loops.

6. Lay out your rain fly, making sure the openings of the fly line up with the doors of your tent.

7. Secure the rain fly to the tent frame, and stake it down.

When you're ready to head home, pack your tent in the same order you take it down: rain fly, tent, and ground tarp. This way, when you set it up again, everything unpacks in the order you will need it. Let wet tents dry out before packing them away.

TRY THIS! Practice building simple shelters at home using furniture, blankets, pillows, and yarn.

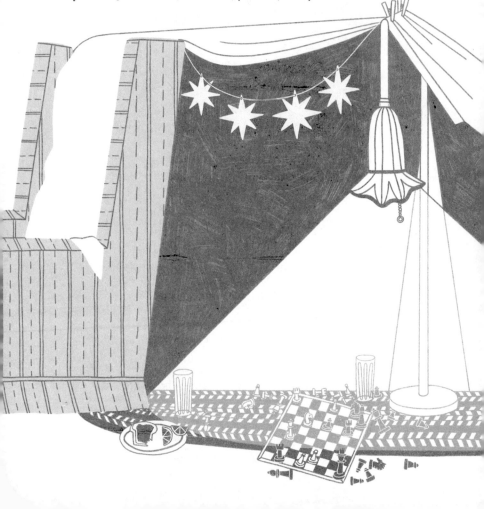

Tents aren't the only kind of common outdoor shelter; it can be fun to stay in a cabin, hut, or camper. In winter, some people build snow shelters. Before we had reliable tents, campers built small shelters using fallen branches, grasses, and other materials near their campsites. Other common kinds of outdoor shelters are cabins, yurts, lean-tos, snow structures, and campers.

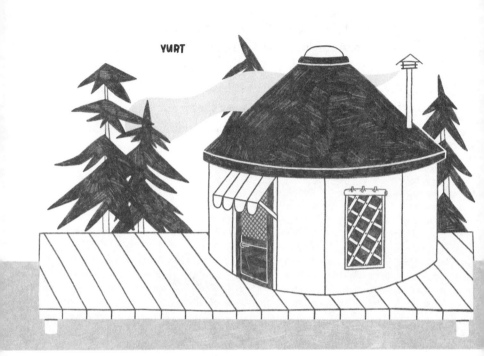

YURT

CAMPER

A-FRAME

IGLOO

TARP GEAR BURRITO

TENT-SHADE TARP

DID YOU KNOW? Inuits, an indigenous people of Canada, Greenland, and Alaska, have been building winter shelters for thousands of years using blocks of snow or ice as bricks. *Quinzhees* (say "kwINzis") are snow structures similar to igloos, but they are made from hollowed-out mounds of snow.

Tarps

Tarps are sturdy sheets of waterproof material designed to be secured with rope by holes along their edges. You can hang tarps in your campsite to make dry areas in rainy weather. In fact, tarps are some of the most useful things to bring camping. Here's a list of things to use your tarp for:

- Rain cover
- Sunshade
- Tent
- Gear storage
- Ground cover

SUNSHADE TARP

TYING A KNOT

If you do need to hang a tarp, you're going to need to know at least one good knot. The half hitch knot is one of the most useful knots to know how to tie, especially if you're trying to attach something to a post or tree (like your tarp or hammock). Here's how: loop the rope around your post, loop one end around the line, and pull the end through the newly formed loop. Repeat for a stronger knot!

SINGLE HALF HITCH   DOUBLE HALF HITCH

Build a Tarp Shelter

Once you've practiced building some shelters inside, you can try building one outdoors at home or in your campsite. The instructions here are for a lean-to-style shelter. When you've mastered it, try to build a different style on your own! You can read more about outdoor shelters in the classic book from 1920 by Daniel Carter Beard, *Shelters, Shacks, and Shanties*. And remember, never cut down healthy plants or tree limbs to build a shelter; they are already someone else's home.

WHAT YOU'LL NEED:
A tree, rock, wall, or other sturdy thing to act as a base
Twine, rope, or nylon cord
Tent stakes
Camping tarp

WHAT TO DO:

1. Choose a site and a tree, rock, or other large, tall thing to use as a base.

2. Attach a piece of twine, rope, or nylon cord to one corner of your tarp.

3. Loop the other end around the tree (or large thing) as high as you can reach. Secure it with a half hitch knot.

CONTINUED

4. Tie another line with a small loop at the end to the opposite corner of your tarp, and secure the looped end to the ground with a tent stake so the tarp is pulled tight.

5. Pull out the other two corners, attach additional line as needed, and stake them to the ground with tent stakes.

FIRE

· · · · · · · · · ·

Building a fire is one of the most important outdoor skills you can learn. Campfires are used for light, heat, and cooking, and they are where people gather to talk, tell stories, and sing songs. It is important to always have an adult with you when you are anywhere near a fire.

Before You Build Your Fire

1. Find out the fire danger level in the area where you are camping. The US Forest Service and most campgrounds post the fire danger level. Build fires only when the fire danger is low or moderate.

2. Build or clean out the fire ring. A fire ring is a shallow pit dug into the ground and ringed with stones or metal to keep the fire contained. If there is no pit or fire ring, check to make sure it is allowed to build a fire, then dig a shallow pit, collect stones, and place them around the edges of the pit.

3. Make sure your fire is away from trees, shrubs, grasses, or tents that could catch stray sparks.

Building Your Fire

There are lots of different ways to stack wood in a pit to make a fire, but they all share one thing in common—they have the smallest pieces toward the middle and the larger pieces to the outside. Here are step-by-step instructions for building a fire in any kind of weather, using the tepee method.

1. Collect kindling and wood. You want sticks of all different sizes; a couple of big handfuls of dry needles, leaves, moss, or paper for tinder; and at least two good logs. Keep your wood dry and away from the fire pit.

2. Place a handful-sized pile of tinder in the center of the fire pit and begin propping successively larger tepees of sticks around it.

3. Add larger pieces of kindling to the structure, leaving a small opening on one side to light the tinder.

4. Place two or three smaller logs on the outside of the structure, leaning them against one another for support.

5. Light the tinder at the base of your structure.

TEPEE

LOG CABIN

Other fire structures are useful depending on the weather and how you plan to use your fire. Fire structures with square bottoms that you can rest a pan on are good for cooking, and fires built like lean-tos (with tiny roofs) are good in the rain.

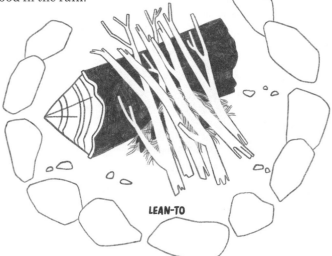

LEAN-TO

Tips for a Successful Fire

- Use dry wood.
- Face the opening of your tepee away from the wind.
- Leave room for air.
- Use lots of dry kindling.
- Use a fire starter (see Create Cardboard-Coil Fire Starters below).

Create Cardboard-Coil Fire Starters

Fire starters are special kinds of kindling, usually about the size of a fist, that help a fire get started by burning easily and slowly. This fire starter is small and should be made at home several days before you want to build your fire.

WHAT YOU'LL NEED:

Scissors
Noncorrugated cardboard (like from a cereal box)
Pencil or pen
Masking or scotch tape
3- or 4-inch-across metal jar lid (like from a pickle jar)
Aluminum foil
Kitchen knife
Old candle (about ¼ cup wax)
Small glass mixing bowl
3 cups water
Medium-sized pot

WHAT TO DO:

1. Cut a 1-inch-wide strip of cardboard that's about 12 inches long. Roll the strip into a coil around a pencil or pen.

2. Let the coil naturally release until it reaches about 2 inches across. Tape the end of the coil to itself to prevent further expansion.

3. Clean and wash a jar lid. Line the inside of the lid with two rectangular layers of aluminum foil, leaving a long wing on either side.

4. Press your coil into the lined lid, and set aside.

5. With the help of an adult, cut an old candle into pea-sized chunks.

6. Line the glass mixing bowl with several layers of foil before placing the wax in the bowl. Heat the water in the pot and bring it to a gentle boil, placing the glass bowl over it as a double boiler.

CONTINUED

7. When the wax is melted, pour it over the top of your coil, filling the bottom of the lid to about ¼ inch. Let this cool for about an hour to set the bottom of your starter.

8. Finish filling the coil with wax, leaving about ⅛ to ¼ inch of cardboard at the top. Let set for 2 hours. Remove it from the jar lid and wrap the wings around your fire starter to pack and transport.

9. At camp, unwrap and light the exposed cardboard end before setting it at the base of your fire.

Fire Safety

Fires are great, but they can also be dangerous. Here's a list of dos and don'ts whenever you have a fire at camp.

- **DO** have adult supervision and permission.

- **DO** keep a bucket of water nearby.

- **DON'T** leave a fire unattended.

- **DO** keep your fire inside your fire pit.

- **DON'T** burn garbage or anything made of plastic or metal.

- **DO** keep toys, chairs, and other tripping hazards away from the fire.

- **DON'T** run around or roughhouse near the fire.

If you do catch a stray spark and your clothing starts to burn, remember to *stop, drop,* and *roll.*

PUTTING IT OUT

Just as important as building a fire is making sure that you put it out—completely. The ideal way to put out a fire is with plenty of water. Pour a large amount of water over the fire, wait a few minutes, stir it in with a stick, and then do it all over again.

The most important reason to be sure that your fire is out is to prevent forest fires. Forest fires from campsites burn millions of acres of national forests every year. These big fires destroy animal homes and fragile forest communities that are hundreds or even thousands of years old. Preventing forest fires is so important that the US Forest Service has been using Smokey Bear to remind us about fire safety for more than 75 years! Smokey was a real little bear cub that was rescued from a forest fire in 1950. He recovered and became the symbol for preventing fires. When you enter a national forest, look for Forest Service signs with Smokey telling you what the fire danger is. If it's high, it's not a good day for a fire.

DID YOU KNOW? Small forest fires caused by natural things like lightning are actually good for forests. Some plants need fires for their seeds to sprout, while others rely on fires to clear out choking brush.

CLARE MARIE HODGES
The First Female National Park Ranger

Clare Marie Hodges grew up in Santa Cruz, California,
and first encountered Yosemite National Park on a 4-day
horse-riding excursion when she was 14 years old. Right
away, she fell in love. In 1918, when most American men
were away at war, she started work as a park ranger in
Yosemite after completing 2 years of training. Unlike other
female park employees, who worked mostly in office and
customer-service jobs until the 1970s, Clare rode the range
and had the same responsibilities as the male rangers.
With one big exception—she never carried a gun on her
patrols. She remained the only fully commissioned female
park ranger for 30 years. Nowadays, although women make
up more than half the US population, only about 30 percent
of park rangers are women.

Test Your Fire-Safety Smarts

Take this quiz, using a separate piece of paper, to see if you've mastered your fire skills. Once you've passed it, teach what you've learned to a friend. Can they pass it too?

1. Fires can be built a) anywhere, anytime; b) only when it's raining; c) when the Forest Service says it's okay.

2. The safest place to build a fire is a) in a fire ring; b) in a grassy field; c) by a stream.

3. The best way to put out a fire is a) with water; b) by burying it; c) by letting it burn down.

4. True or false: All forest fires are bad.

5. True or false: It's okay to leave your fire burning while you sleep in your tent at night.

6. The safest way to get your fire to be hot is to a) slowly add logs to build a bed of coals; b) fan it; c) throw trash on it.

7. Extra wood and kindling should be kept a) in your tent; b) away from stray sparks; c) close to the fire ring.

8. It's safe to burn a) disposable plates and cups; b) wood and tinder; c) pop cans and aluminum foil.

9. If you accidentally catch on fire, the first thing to do is a) run around screaming; b) stop, drop, and roll; c) run to the nearest river.

10. The campfire is a great place to a) run around and roughhouse; b) leave toys and sports equipment; c) sing songs.

ANSWER KEY: 1. c; 2. a; 3. a; 4. false; 5. false; 6. a; 7. b; 8. b; 9. b; 10. c

CHAPTER 6

GOOD GRUB

Bananas of the world: unite!

Peel, banana,

Peel peel, banana,

Shake, banana,

Shake shake, banana,

Go, bananas!

Go go, bananas!

—CAMP CHANT

Food and water are two of the most important things to bring with you outside. They give you energy, help maintain your body temperature, and keep you in good spirits. Being able to cook a delicious meal for friends and family while at camp is a wonderful way to contribute to your group. All of the recipes in this chapter are simple and fun; some of them are meant to be started or made before you set out, but most of them can be cooked right in camp.

BEFORE YOU COOK

Camp kitchens, like kitchens at home, are places to be careful. At camp, since you don't have a refrigerator or hot running water, it's even more important to keep your hands and cooking surfaces clean, to keep cold foods cold in ice-filled coolers, and to use sharp or hot things with the help of a responsible adult.

> **TRY THIS!** Keep your drinks cool in a stream by placing them in a plastic bag and tying the top with cord or rope. Secure the other end to a rock or tree to make sure they don't float away.

Bears and Other Hungry Things

You are not the only one at camp who thinks your food smells delicious. Squirrels and birds love anything with nuts or seeds and will forage through your pack to get to them. Larger animals, like cougars and bears, may be drawn by the smell of cooking bacon or a delicious burger. These big animals rarely come near people and are almost always more interested in your food than they are in you.

Tips for keeping the critters away:

- Store food in plastic containers and bags.

- Keep food far away from your tent.

- Check your backpack and pockets for garbage and leftover snacks when you return to camp.

- Keep a clean camp kitchen, always remembering to pick up scraps and do dishes.

- At night, make sure your food is out of reach, usually in a high tree.

- Read and follow all rules and posted signs about wildlife and food safety.

How to hang your food:

1. Tie or tape one end of a long piece of rope to a shoe.

2. Tie the other end of the rope to your food bag.

3. Toss the shoe over the branch.

4. Pull down on the shoe end of the rope, raising the bag into the air as high as you can.

5. Tie the rope around the trunk of the tree using two half hitch knots (see page 94).

You may not always be able to hang your food. Sometimes the trees are too big, or too far apart, or just not there at all. Don't worry! You can use a sturdy metal bear canister too, and most campsites in bear country have bear boxes—big metal containers for food storage that bears can't open.

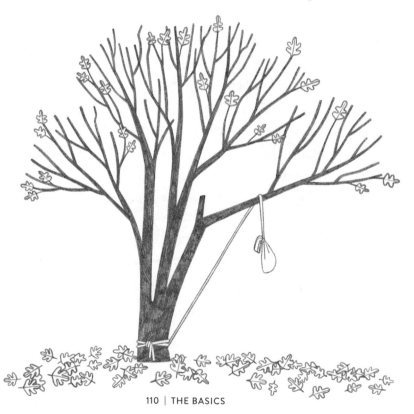

HOW TO COOK OUTDOORS

The most fun way to cook at camp is right over the campfire, which you should always do with the help of an adult. Fires used for cooking need to have a good bed of hot coals to cook over. These coals form over time as the fire uses up larger pieces of wood, so cooking fires need to be started long before you want to cook. It's also important that a cooking fire isn't so big that you might burn yourself reaching for a pot or lost potato. Most official campsite rings have a heavy metal grate for cooking that heats as it sits atop the fire. If you are cooking in a pan, you can test if the fire is hot enough by warming the pan on the grate for a few minutes and then sprinkling the pan with water. If it's hot enough, the droplets will jump and sizzle when they hit the pan!

The easiest way to cook over an open fire is to put whatever you want to cook on a stick and hold it in the flames. Try to find a damp stick that won't easily catch on fire. You can have an adult help you shave the end into a fine point with a pocketknife.

Five things to cook on a stick:

1. Bagels
2. Sausages
3. Bananas (in the peel)
4. Marshmallows
5. Bacon

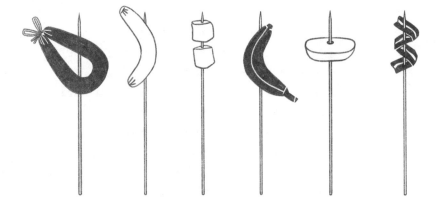

> **TRY THIS!** Make a cinnamon twist by wrapping premade cinnamon-bun dough around your stick before roasting.

Just as easy but not quite as much fun is to wrap whatever you want to cook in aluminum foil and nestle it in the coals. This works best on foods too hard (or big) to fit on a stick.

Five things to cook in foil:

1. Baked potatoes
2. Corn on the cob
3. Mushrooms
4. Fresh-caught fish
5. Apple chunks with sugar and cinnamon

BACKPACKING STOVE

Portable Stoves

When you camp, you'll probably bring your own portable stove to cook on that burns gas (such as propane) for fuel instead of wood, rather than relying on a campfire. These kinds of portable stoves were invented in the 1800s, but people have been using other kinds of portable stoves that burned wood and other materials for fuel for a very long time.

TWO-BURNER STOVE

DID YOU KNOW? *Shichirin* are portable charcoal-burning stoves made of clay; they were used as early as the 1600s in Japan.

SHICHIRIN STOVE

Build a Traveler's Stove and Burner

Before the first commercial camp stoves were invented, travelers and campers had to invent their own designs for portable stoves using whatever materials were nearby. Many of these makeshift stoves were made from discarded metal cans and buckets—an early example of reuse and recycle. Follow the instructions below to make your own traveler's stove and burner. Note: Your traveler's stove does not get hot enough to cook poultry!

**WHAT YOU'LL NEED
FOR THE BURNER:**
Scissors
Noncorrugated cardboard (like
   from a cereal box)
Pencil or pen
Masking or scotch tape
One 4-ounce metal can (like a
   tuna can)
Kitchen knife
Old candle (about ¼ cup wax)

Small glass mixing bowl
Aluminum foil
3 cups water
Medium-sized pot

**WHAT YOU'LL NEED
FOR THE STOVE:**
Can opener
1 large metal can (coffee cans
   work best)
Tin snips or sturdy scissors

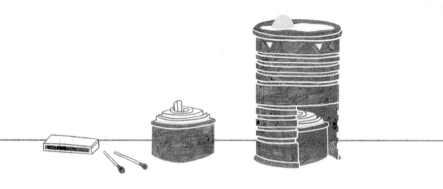

WHAT TO DO:

1. To make the burner, cut a 1-inch-wide strip of cardboard that's about 12 inches long. Roll the strip into a coil around a pencil or pen.

2. Let the coil naturally release until it reaches about 2 inches across. Tape the end of the coil to itself to prevent further expansion.

3. Place your cardboard coil into the center of your cleaned, dry can.

4. With the help of an adult, cut an old candle into pea-sized chunks.

5. Line the glass mixing bowl with several layers of foil before placing the wax in the bowl. Heat the water in the pot and bring it to a gentle boil, placing the glass bowl over it as a double boiler.

6. When the wax is melted, pour it over the coil, filling the can to within ¼ inch of the top.

7. Allow to cool overnight.

CONTINUED

8. To make the stove, remove plastic cap (if using coffee can) or use can opener to remove one metal end of the large can. Wash and dry it, removing the label. The remaining end will be your burner.

9. Turn the can upside down, so the closed end is up and the open end is down.

10. Using the can opener, punch several holes in the sides of the can, near the top.

11. Using tin snips or sturdy scissors, cut a 4-by-4-inch square into the bottom of one side of the can.

12. When you're ready to cook, light the exposed cardboard end of your burner and place your stove over the top. Remember, some burners last longer than others (based on the kind of wax and cardboard you use), so if you are planning on cooking more than one meal on your stove, bring more than one burner!

MEASUREMENTS AND STANDARDS FOR OUTDOOR COOKING

In a normal recipe, the ingredients are all measured out exactly, so that you know precisely how it will turn out each time. It's the same thing with cooking times and temperatures. At home, we have timers and oven settings that let us cook something for exactly half an hour at

350 degrees Fahrenheit. In the wild, especially if you're cooking over a fire, there's a lot of guesswork. This handy guide should make it easier.

Girl's Guide to Outdoor Cooking

COOK TIME: The amount of time needed to make the food look and smell done. Most outdoor cooking takes longer than cooking at home. For many foods, like red meat, it is easy to tell when they are done (when all redness is gone). Other foods, like potatoes, may need to be poked with a fork to see if they are soft.

COOKING TEMPERATURES: Instead of listing temperatures, outdoor recipes will tell you where to place the food to be cooked: directly over the hottest part of the fire or coals for high temperatures, overlapping the flames for medium heats, or to the side of the fire for low temperatures.

MEASUREMENTS: The recipes included in this book all list exact measurements, but if you find yourself without a set of measuring spoons or cups outdoors, you can use these guidelines:

- A big pinch: About 1 teaspoon
- A small handful: About ¼ cup
- A big handful: About ½ cup
- Two big handfuls: About 1 cup
- To taste: As much as tastes good to you

Snack Recipes

When you're hiking, climbing, or riding, you can burn more than 300 calories an hour, so it's important to snack as you go. Outdoor snacks should be easy to carry and clean up. These snacks can all be prepared in advance of your trip.

Real Fruit Rolls

Dehydrated foods are foods that have been dried to remove their water. They can be stored safely for a long period of time and can stand up to very hot and very cold temperatures, so they are popular foods for camping. Fruit rolls are made out of mashed and dehydrated fruits. Since some of the earliest people to dry food lived in the Middle East, this recipe uses a common fruit from that region, figs. You can also make this recipe using a berry or a hard fruit, like apples, pears, or peaches, that is common where you live.

Makes about 12 rolls

INGREDIENTS:
4 cups peeled and diced apples
2 cups diced figs
Pinch of ground cinnamon
3 tablespoons agave syrup
½ cup water

EQUIPMENT:
Saucepan
Blender
Parchment paper
Cookie sheet
Pizza cutter
String
Plastic bag

TO COOK:

1. Preheat the oven to 170 degrees F (or your lowest oven setting).

2. Place the apples, figs, cinnamon, syrup, and water in a saucepan over medium heat and cover. Simmer for 15 to 20 minutes. Turn off the heat and let cool completely.

3. Pour the fruit into a blender and blend until smooth.

4. Spread the mixture onto a parchment-paper-lined cookie sheet. Bake for 2 to 3 hours. The rolls should be leathery and moldable, but not sticky or brittle, when done. Cool them and cut into strips with a pizza cutter, then roll up each strip and tie it with a piece of string. Place in a plastic bag for storage.

GORP: The Ultimate Trail Mix

GORP is what most outdoor people call "trail mix." GORP stands for "good old raisins and peanuts," which was what most early trail mixes contained. Now, trail mix can be any combination of nuts, dried fruits, seeds, and chocolate.

Makes 6 servings

INGREDIENTS:
½ cup salted peanuts
½ cup salted cashews
¼ cup M&M's
⅓ cup raisins
⅓ cup dried cranberries
¼ cup sunflower seeds

EQUIPMENT:
Large bowl
Resealable sandwich bags

TO MAKE:

1. Combine the peanuts, cashews, M&M's, raisins, cranberries, and sunflower seeds in a large bowl and mix thoroughly. Store in resealable sandwich bags.

TIP: Mix and match your favorite nuts and dried fruits to create your own signature trail mix.

Popcorn Campfire Satchels

Some foods are just plain fun, and these sweet and salty popcorn satchels are one of them. Make these packets ahead of time and leave plenty of room for the kernels to expand.

Makes 4 servings

INGREDIENTS:
4 cups popcorn kernels
4 tablespoons brown sugar
4 pinches of salt and pepper
4 tablespoons butter

EQUIPMENT:
Scissors
Aluminum foil

TO COOK:

1. Cut (or tear) four large squares of aluminum foil that are about the size of dinner plates.

2. Holding a foil square cupped in one hand, pour about a cup of kernels into the depression.

3. Sprinkle 1 tablespoon of brown sugar and a pinch of salt and pepper over the kernels.

4. Gather the corners of the foil and twist them together, making a little balloon shape and leaving about 3 inches of air at the top.

5. Repeat with the remaining foil squares.

CONTINUED

6. Just before placing them in the fire, open each satchel and put about a tablespoon of butter on top of the kernels.

7. Finally, reseal the satchels and place them on a grill over the fire or on a bed of coals. Listen for the sound of popping. You will know your satchels are done when you can count to 10 between each pop.

Meals

All the recipes here for meals are familiar foods designed to be made at camp, and most of them can be cooked on a traveler's stove (see page 114). If you don't have your traveler's stove, don't worry! You can cook all the meals using regular pots and pans over a fire or camp stove too.

Traveler's Blueberry Flapjacks

Flapjacks might be one of the earliest hiking foods. Evidence of flat cakes made out of ground grains were found with Ötzi the Iceman, who scientists believe traveled long distances over the Swiss Alps more than 5,000 years ago. For this modern-day version, you can combine the dry ingredients at home to save time. Dot the blueberries onto the flapjacks as they cook to make any design you like. If you make these on your traveler's stove, you won't even need a pan!

Makes 4 to 6 servings

INGREDIENTS:
3 tablespoons butter,
    plus more for cooking
1½ cups milk
2 tablespoons sugar
½ teaspoon salt
½ teaspoon ground cinnamon
1½ cups flour
1½ teaspoons baking powder
1 to 2 cups blueberries
Jam, for a topping

EQUIPMENT:
Traveler's stove or camp
    stove with a frying pan
Large bowl
Aluminum foil

TO COOK:

1. Light and allow your traveler's stove to warm for about 5 minutes, preparing it with a small amount of butter.

CONTINUED

2. In a large bowl, whisk together the milk, sugar, salt, and cinnamon. Stir in the flour and baking powder.

3. Carefully spoon just enough batter onto the clean surface of your stove to cover the burner, leaving about a finger's width of space around the edge.

4. Cook each flapjack until bubbles form on the surface, then dot with blueberries. Flip over, and cook for about 1 minute more. Remove each flapjack from the stove and place in a stack in foil to keep warm near the morning fire, or serve each flapjack hot off the stove. Serve with jam.

Brown-Bag Eggs and Bacon

Good things can come in very simple packages, or in this case, in humble brown bags. Variations on the brown-bag breakfast have been around the campfire for generations because of the easy preparation and cleanup. In this recipe, the butter keeps the bag from catching fire.

Makes 4 servings

INGREDIENTS:
Butter (for greasing the bags)
8 slices bacon
4 eggs
Salt and pepper, to taste

EQUIPMENT:
4 paper lunch bags
4 sticks

TO COOK:

1. Coat the inside of each bag with plenty of butter.

2. Lay two slices of bacon across the bottom of one bag. Crack an egg onto the bacon, add salt and pepper, and fold the top of the bag down three times. Repeat with the remaining bags.

3. Poke a stick through the top of each bag and hold over the fire until the eggs are firm. Be careful not to get your bag too close to the flames, or you may burn your breakfast!

Peanut Butter, Banana, and Honey Sandwiches

Peanut butter sandwiches are the unsung heroes of outdoor adventurers. They are sturdy, packed with healthy calories, and stay fresh in any kind of weather. This version adds an extra boost of potassium from the banana to help ease sore muscles.

Makes 4 servings

INGREDIENTS:
2 medium-sized bananas
4 tablespoons peanut butter
2 tablespoons honey
8 slices multigrain sandwich
  bread

EQUIPMENT:
Knife

TO MAKE:

1. Peel and slice the bananas into rounds. Spread about a tablespoon of peanut butter and a ½ tablespoon of honey onto four of the slices of bread. Cover with banana rounds and top each sandwich with another bread slice.

2. Make up your own peanut butter sandwich recipe by adding things like raisins, strawberries, jam, or even bacon.

Fire-Grilled Cheese Sandwiches

These easy-to-assemble sandwiches are best gooey and eaten right off the fire. They can be made with any type of cheese you prefer.

Makes 4 servings

INGREDIENTS:
4 tablespoons butter
8 slices multigrain sandwich
   bread
8 thick slices cheddar cheese
1 large tomato, sliced into
   8 pieces

EQUIPMENT:
Knife
Spatula

TO COOK:

1. Butter the outside of each piece of bread. Place two slices of cheese and two slices of tomato on each sandwich, gently pressing them closed.

2. Use a camp toaster, the grate out of your own backyard barbecue, or a portable kitchen grill rack to toast the sandwiches over the fire, flipping them with a spatula when the cheese starts to melt. When both sides are golden brown, they're done!

Traveler's Burritos with Fire-Toasted Tortillas

Burritos, Spanish for "little donkeys," are a traditional food from Mexico of beans, rice, meat, and cheese wrapped in a tortilla. This recipe packs a lot of taste into a tiny package with hot sauce and lime.

Makes 4 servings

INGREDIENTS:
1 can refried beans
1 large tomato
1 avocado
1 cup cheddar cheese
2 limes
4 tortillas
Hot sauce, to taste
¼ cup sour cream

EQUIPMENT:
Pot
Traveler's stove
Knife
Cutting board
Small bowls, for serving
Tongs
Aluminum foil

TO COOK:

1. In a pot over low heat, warm the beans, stirring them every few minutes.

2. While the beans heat, chop the tomato, cut open and slice the avocado, grate the cheese, and cut the limes into quarters. Set each of the ingredients out on a cutting board or in their own small bowls for self-service.

3. Once the beans are warm, remove them from the heat and place near the service bar. With tongs, grab your tortilla and toast it over the fire like a marshmallow. Other ways to heat your tortillas are to lay them on a grill and turn them or to wrap several together in aluminum foil and place in the coals (this option is perfect for large groups).

4. Fill each tortilla with beans, tomatoes, avocados, and cheese. Squeeze some lime over the top and add hot sauce and sour cream before rolling them up.

TRY THIS! Make campfire nachos from your leftover beans and cheese by putting them on tortilla chips nested in foil and heating in the fire.

Traveler's Burgers

While most Americans think of beef when they hear "burger," other countries have different main ingredients for their "hot-bunned sandwiches." In Russia and Germany pork burgers are common, while in India chicken and bean patties are the most common. For this recipe, use whichever patty sounds easy and delicious (although if you choose to use chicken, you'll need to cook it over a camp stove or the fire, as your traveler's stove will not get hot enough to safely cook poultry).

Makes 4 servings

INGREDIENTS:
1 tomato
4 thin (¼-inch) beef, pork, grain,
    or bean patties
Salt and pepper, to taste
4 whole-grain burger buns or
    sturdy rolls
4 to 8 slices cheddar cheese
1 jar sliced dill pickles
Ketchup, for serving
Mustard, for serving

EQUIPMENT:
Traveler's stove
Knife

TO COOK:

1. Set up and light your traveler's stove. Allow the stove to heat for about 5 minutes while you slice the tomato, setting it on a separate surface away from your meat.

2. Cook each patty one at a time on your stove until it is juicy and brown all the way through. Season with salt and pepper just before taking off the heat. Toast the buns over the fire or over your camp stove.

3. Dress your burgers with cheese, tomato, pickles, ketchup, and mustard. Enjoy!

REMEMBER: Your traveler's stove doesn't get hot enough to safely cook poultry!

1-1-1 Chocolate Camp Fondue

This fun and easy dessert is designed for groups of any size, and it's easy to remember the recipe—just use equal amounts of each of the ingredients! To make more fondue, just increase the amounts, making sure to use equal portions.

Makes 4 to 6 servings

INGREDIENTS:
½ cup Nutella
½ cup semisweet chocolate chips
½ cup condensed milk

INGREDIENTS FOR DIPPING:
¼ cup nuts (almonds, walnuts, or hazelnuts are best), chopped, for coating
2 to 3 graham crackers, crumbled, for coating
2 to 3 graham crackers, broken into rectangles
2 cups strawberries, bananas, or apples (or all three), sliced
1 to 2 cups large marshmallows

EQUIPMENT:
Camp stove
Pot
Bowl
Knife
Small bowls and dipping tray, for serving

TO COOK:

1. Fill a pot about halfway full with water and bring to a boil.

2. Place the Nutella, chocolate chips, and milk in a heat-proof glass or metal bowl, and nest the bowl in the pot to create a double boiler. Slowly melt the chocolate, stirring continuously. When it is fully mixed and melted, remove from the heat to cool for 3 to 5 minutes.

3. While it is cooling, set out your dipping tray, arranging the nuts and crumbled graham crackers for coating in separate small bowls alongside the graham cracker rectangles, fruit, and marshmallows for dipping. Dip and enjoy!

TRY THIS! Record your favorite outdoor recipes in your field journal or on notecards for your camp activity bin. Include a list of ingredients, instructions, and notes on where and when you cooked them.

QUENCHING YOUR THIRST

More than half your body is made up of water, so it's pretty important to keep replacing all the fluids you lose from working and playing hard outside. On a hot day, you might need to drink more than ten glasses of water just to replace all that sweat! If you don't drink enough water, it can make you crabby, give you a headache, and make you feel generally icky (maybe achy, maybe queasy; it can be hard to describe). When that happens, it's called dehydration. So, if it's hot out and you find yourself feeling sick or arguing with your best friend for no reason, take a break to drink a full glass of water and see if it helps.

You can help yourself avoid dehydration in the first place by drinking plenty of water before you go. This means that you should drink water the night before and the morning of your departure. You'll know you are drinking enough water when your pee is more clear than yellow.

While it can be tempting to drink from a clear mountain stream, it's not a good idea to drink untreated water from a stream or other body of water. Even clean-looking water contains all sorts of things, from sand and silt to bacteria, that can make you sick. When you're outside, it's important to treat your water with iodine, special ultraviolet lights, or a filter to make it safe to drink.

TRY THIS! Turn your water into a tasty and frosty beverage by adding your favorite drink powder. Fill your bottle three-quarters full so it doesn't burst, then put it in the freezer for 8 hours before heading out. It will melt as you go!

DID YOU KNOW? You should never drink seawater, no matter how thirsty you are. Our kidneys can flush out only a certain amount of salt at a time, so the salt from seawater forces us to use up more water than we drink, making us dangerously thirsty.

MESS DUTY

No cooking task is complete until the mess you made is cleaned up. Doing dishes, wiping down surfaces, and putting away all the kitchen items are extra important outside, so that you don't draw critters to camp. Cleaning up is also a good way to say thank you when someone else has done the cooking. It's okay to use stream water to wash dishes (save your treated water for drinking, cooking, and toothbrushing).

FANNIE FARMER
Inventor of the Standard Measure

In the late 1800s, Fannie Farmer introduced the idea of taking a scientific approach to cooking by using standardized measurements (teaspoons, cups, etc.) in recipes; before that, most recipes were written out as long stories, with little information about amounts, times, or temperatures. A recipe from the early 1800s might suggest simply cooking a chicken with water, carrots, onions, and spices instead of listing the exact types, amounts, and preparation of each ingredient in a chicken soup. Fannie also pioneered cooking equipment designed for people with special physical needs. She's the reason we all have measuring cups and spoons today! When she was 16, she suffered a stroke that left her unable to walk, but after many years of hard work, she recovered and was able to attend the Boston Cooking School, which she eventually took over as director. She is best known for her book *The Boston Cooking-School Cook Book*, which was first published in 1896 and is still used today.

CHAPTER 7

GIRL STUFF

Do your ears hang low? Do they wobble to and fro?

Can you tie them in a knot? Can you tie them in a bow?

—CAMP SONG

Outside is the perfect place to practice being you, and not just any version of you: the very best version. When you're outside is the time to forget about how you look, especially since *everybody's* hair looks super goofy on a windy day or after being smooshed by a helmet. Or, better yet, decide that you do, in fact, look your best when you are on an adventure, being brave, helpful, and curious. Because it's true. It's also a good idea to remind yourself that throwing, dressing, or acting "like a girl" is a good thing. So is being a girl who doesn't look or act "like a girl." The world needs all kinds of girls, and there's no one kind of person who gets to be an outdoor adventurer. You know how to become an outdoor adventurer? By going outdoors.

HOW TO GET DRESSED

Getting dressed when you're outside can be awkward. Especially if you can't stand up in your tent, you're trying to keep your feet clean, or it's super cold outside. Here are some tricks for getting dressed in every happenstance.

- On a day hike: Change in the car.

- At a picnic, the beach, or by the lake: Change in the bushes, behind a tree, log, or big rock.

- When your feet are wet: Change on a ground tarp outside your tent.

- In a group: Change under your clothes (bring an extra skirt for day trips and pull it on over any clothes you want to take off, so you're covered), or use a towel to wrap around yourself and change under that.

- When it's freezing: Change inside your sleeping bag.

TRY THIS! See if you can change your clothes inside your sleeping bag in less than a minute.

BATHING

· · · · · · · · · · · · · · · ·

Outside is a dirty place! If you are having a lot of fun, then you are likely to get very dirty and maybe a little bit stinky too. If you are outdoors for just a day or two, you might be able to wait to clean up until you get home. But if you are going to be gone for longer (or get *super* dirty), try one of these ways to clean up.

SPIT BATHS: For short trips or dry camping conditions, a quick and simple wipe down with moist towelettes or a damp cloth will do the trick until you get home. This is called a "spit bath" even though you (thankfully) don't use spit.

NATURAL WATERS: Long before there were showers and indoor plumbing, there was bathing in the nearest stream or lake, and it's still the most fun way to get clean outside. Just make sure you use soap that's safe for fish, too, by finding brands that use natural ingredients and are biodegradable.

SOLAR SHOWERS: Solar showers are basically thick rubber water sacks that warm in the sunlight and are then hung from a line or tree limb, so you can shower in the heated water using the attached tubing and showerhead.

Five reasons to leave makeup at home:

1. It melts.

2. It freezes.

3. It comes open.

4. It smears.

5. It keeps you from putting on sunscreen.

HAIR

· · · · · · · · · · ·

Everyone's hair is different, and regardless of what kind of texture it is—tight, frizzy, curly, straight, thick, thin, oily, dry—any kind of hair can be a challenge to manage outside. Even cutting it super short has its challenges—since hair helps keep our head warm, people with very short hair need to remember to bring a hat!

The goal for outdoor hair is to keep it as clean and tidy and out of the way as possible. When you choose a hairstyle, consider your planned activities. If you will need to wear a helmet or hat, it is best to pull long hair back and down into a braid or low bun or ponytail. While it might be tempting to use a lot of hairspray or gel to hold your hair in place, remember that you might not get to shower every day, or maybe even at all. All that product can turn your hair into one big, dirty rat's nest if you don't get a chance to wash it out. In general, if you like to use hair products, try to choose natural products, since they work on all kinds of hair textures, are easier to wash out, and get less grimy than other products when you're heading outside.

Five great braided hairstyles:

1. Pippi braids
2. Heidi braids
3. French braids
4. Braided ponytail
5. Braided top bun (if you won't be wearing a helmet or other hat)

BRAIDED TOP BUN   **HEIDI BRAID**   **BRAIDED PONYTAIL**

Another way of taming and taking care of your hair is to use a headband, hat, or scarf of some kind. This also helps prevent your scalp from burning (if you don't wear a hat or scarf, be sure to put sunscreen on your part and hairline). Head scarves and kerchiefs have been used to protect hair and keep women and men cool in the sun for thousands of years by people from all over the world. If you always wear a head scarf, there are versions designed especially for sports and the outdoors that are waterproof, breathable, and stay put. In the winter it's easiest to just cover your hair with a beanie—it's warmer that way, anyhow.

Four ways to tie a head scarf:

1. Under tied on top
2. Over tied on bottom
3. As a headband
4. As a wrap

OVER TIED ON BOTTOM   **HEADBAND**   **UNDER TIED ON TOP**

HOW TO PEE (AND POOP) IN THE WOODS

When a girl's gotta go, a girl's gotta go. Even when there isn't a particularly fabulous place to go. Sometimes especially then. It's okay; everyone worries a little about going outside at first, because it's not something we do every day. But not so long ago, it used to be. The first bathrooms were shallow holes, just like the holes dug by cats, and that's the best way for humans to go outside too. You can use either the heel of your shoe or a hand trowel to dig a cat hole, and, just like a cat, kick some dirt or debris over it when you're done. Whether you're peeing or pooping in the outdoors, the trick to being successful and mess-free is a really good squat. And remember to take your flashlight with you into outhouses and after dark.

Tip: What to Do with the Toilet Paper

Bring toilet paper (more than you think you'll need) and two plastic resealable bags—one for your clean toilet paper and one to pack out the used toilet paper. Keep the bags in your backpack or coat pocket. It might seem gross to carry your used toilet paper around with you, but it's not as gross as leaving it behind for someone else to find (or finding some else's!). You'll find it's a lot easier if you use plenty of toilet paper, so that you can fold it up really well before putting it inside your plastic bag. Never leave toilet paper behind in the wilderness.

DID YOU KNOW?
Outhouses may have been the first true unisex bathrooms! Early outhouses used to mark a moon for women and a star for men, but due to practical reasons in the outdoors, that quickly gave way to the traditional moon and star we still see today.

Six steps to going outside:

1. Find a good place to go that is private, with a large rock or tree that you can hold on to. If you're in a group, designate the bathroom area the group will use. Always try to go at least 100 feet from the nearest stream—and away from your site. That keeps our water and campsites clean for the next campers. If you are on a slope, face uphill. Use your heel or a small trowel to dig a cat hole if you think you might need to go number two.

2. Look around for anything sharp or thorny that might poke you, snow or loose soil that may give way, or dangerous plants, like poison oak or poison ivy (see page 216 for illustrations of these plants).

3. Hold on to something and squat. If you don't have something to hang on to, try a deeper squat, so you sit on your heels.

4. Pull your clothes forward and away from you and go for it!

5. Use the clean toilet paper from your plastic bag. Pull out your second (waste) plastic bag, and put the used toilet paper into it. You can store your waste bag, sealed, inside your clean toilet paper bag. Put your full toilet paper bag into the garbage to be taken out with you at the end of your trip.

6. Wash or sanitize your hands, and cover your cat hole. Done!

TRY THIS! Have you ever thought it might be nice to be able to pee standing up like the boys? It turns out, so did a lot of other girls! Now, there are funnels that let us go without having to squat—they're great for boats and snowy weather! You can find these products online or at outdoor retailers, or make your own from flexible funnels found at the auto parts store.

GETTING YOUR PERIOD

The worst part of getting your period outside is worrying about getting your period outside. In fact, the worst part of getting your period at all might be worrying about getting your period. Once it happens, though, it turns out it's not such a big deal after all. Your body might warn you that it's about to happen with some cramps, or it might not and you go to the bathroom to discover you've started bleeding. If that happens, use some wadded-up toilet paper as a temporary fix until you can get to your pack for some clean clothes and a menstrual product. One good way to stop worrying is to be prepared. Here's how:

- Keep a plastic bag with all your products (pads or tampons, extra toilet paper, etc.) in your day pack, just in case.

- Tell your group leader if you start (or think you might start) your period on a trip. She can help make sure you have time for plenty of bathroom breaks.

- It's okay to sit out some more energetic or water-based activities to read or start a craft project, so don't hesitate to do so if you're feeling under the weather.

Having your period shouldn't keep you at home. If you're worried about it, and especially if it's your first time, talk to your parents, troop leader, other girls, or your doctor or school nurse about your concerns. Even if you are not anticipating your period, plan for it. Some girls start menstruating early and some never have a period. For girls who do, exercise, changes in diet, and being around other girls can shift the timing of your cycle. As you get older, your period will become more predictable.

The Bear Myth

Sometimes people tell tall tales, usually involving giant fish, plants that talk and sing songs, or fairy godmothers with magic shoes. The bear myth is one of those tall tales. Like most tall tales or other campfire stories, there are lots of versions, but this tale always involves a bear attack, and it's always blamed on a girl who had her period. You might hear this story lots of times, and you might be tempted to believe it. Sharks are attracted to the smell of blood, so why wouldn't bears be? And everyone spends so much time worried about the smell of food attracting bears; it seems like maybe bleeding would make it worse.

The truth: *it doesn't.*

There's never been a single proven case of a bear (or any other animal) attacking someone because she was on her period. Period. And that makes sense for a lot of reasons: there's not much blood with your period; it's no more stinky than anything else related to your body, like sweat, pee, or even (maybe especially) poop; and bears, like humans, are attracted to *food*, not waste. They are no more likely to rummage through stinky bathroom trash for food than you are.

So, if you hear this myth, ignore it. The person telling it doesn't know very much about bears or bodies.

> **DID YOU KNOW?** Both grizzly and black bears eat more plants than they do anything else. Look for their berry-filled scat in the middle of summer.

OTHER STUFF ABOUT YOUR BODY

Everybody's body is different. Some of us have hair that gets frizzy in the rain. Some of us grow freckles in the sun. Some of us have big, wide feet that help us to balance. Some of us have really good hearing. All of us eat and poop and blow our noses. However your body is, know that it's just the way it should be for you, and it's the only one you've got, so take really good care of it! Here are a few more body things to know about before you go outside.

Blisters and Hot Spots

Blisters are small, raised pockets of fluid under our skin. We get them when our skin rubs against itself or clothing too much. This happens outside for a lot of reasons: our feet may not be used to hiking long distances, we may have on new shoes or thin socks, or our feet might get wet and rub against the inside of our shoes. But sometimes it seems like it just happens for no real reason, just an off day for your feet. As soon as you start to feel a hot spot forming (it feels like a warm or rubbed place on your foot), it is time to cover it up with an adhesive bandage, some moleskin, or even duct tape.

Hot spots form on other parts of our bodies too. This is especially common in the summer, when our inner thighs and armpits can get red with rubbing. Often, just wearing some nylon or spandex undershorts or rubbing a little petroleum jelly on a hot spot can be an easy fix.

Sunburns

Everyone is at risk for sunburns and skin damage, regardless of their skin color. How long it takes to actually burn will be different for everyone. Put on sunscreen no matter how long you think you will be outside—once before you go out and at least once while you're out. Clothing is even better sun protection than sunscreen. In sunny weather, try a wide-brimmed hat; lightweight, long-sleeved shirt; and lightweight long pants. If you do get burned, try aloe vera gel or a cool, damp cloth to soothe your skin.

DID YOU KNOW? Snow has an especially high *albedo*, meaning it reflects a lot of the sun. The reflection can be bright enough to burn our eyes, causing temporary snow blindness. So, remember those shades even in winter!

Aches and Pains

Adventuring can be hard work. After a long day climbing or riding, it's common to be sore. Leg cramps are the most common, but you can get sore anyplace you use your body. Rock climbers are used to being sore even down to their fingers! Muscle soreness happens because of fatigue and the loss of electrolytes, which are salts that get released with our sweat. Sports drinks are specially designed to replace electrolytes, but salty nuts (see GORP: The Ultimate Trail Mix, page 120) will work too. Drinking water, resting, stretching, and sometimes more moving around can also help muscle soreness.

DID YOU KNOW? Many animals that live in dry climates adapt to store water. The Australian water-holding frog can store enough water in its gills, tissues, and bladder for up to 5 years, and the sandgrouse of northern Africa and central Asia has belly feathers that soak up and store water, so it can be carried back to the bird's nest.

JUDY BLUME
The Barrier Breaker

In the 1970s, Judy Blume started writing books about middle school– and high school–aged girls that talked frankly about what it's like to grow up. In fact, her novels were some of the very first widely read books for girls that included storylines about periods, changes to our bodies during puberty, first relationships, and family issues like divorce. Girls loved her books, but parents, libraries, and politicians thought these topics shouldn't be discussed. For decades (and even sometimes today), books like *Are You There, God? It's Me, Margaret*; *Tiger Eyes*; and *Deenie*, which she wrote to help girls be more comfortable with themselves, were excluded from libraries and banned from schools. But being one of the most censored authors in the United States made her only more determined to fight for girls' rights to talk about their bodies and read stories that reflect their own lives. Judy has become one of the most outspoken champions of free speech in the United States and has never stopped writing books.

PART 3

Advanced Skills

CHAPTER 8

MAPS AND WEATHER

Whether the weather be cold or whether the weather be hot,
We'll weather the weather, whatever the
weather, whether we like it or not.

—CAMP SONG

The most important thing to know about the weather is that *you never really know about the weather,* so come ready for anything, or almost anything. Bring extra layers, extra tarps, and extra sunscreen, and check the weather forecast before you go. This helps you to have a good attitude, whether the weather is good or not.

WHAT MAKES THE WEATHER?

Weather is created by the rotation of the earth, which causes wind, and by the heat from the sun, which causes water to evaporate from the oceans before condensing and falling as rain, hail, or snow over land. Weather is also influenced by masses of cold air from the poles and warm air from the equator meeting and mixing. Regional and local weather is the result of all these things interacting with the features of the landscape, such as lakes, mountains, and plains.

CONDENSATION

PRECIPITATION

EVAPORATION

RUNOFF

WEATHER ESSENTIALS

TEMPERATURE: A measure of how hot or cold something is. We measure temperature in degrees using a thermometer.

ATMOSPHERIC PRESSURE: The weight of air that presses down on any given place on the earth. We measure atmospheric pressure using a barometer. Increasing pressure means sunny weather; decreasing pressure means impending stormy or wet weather.

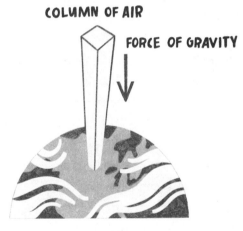

COLUMN OF AIR

FORCE OF GRAVITY

PRECIPITATION: Water, in any form, that falls from clouds. We measure precipitation using a rain gauge or ruler.

WIND: The movement of air across the earth. Wind speed and direction are measured using a weather vane (direction) and anemometer (speed).

THREE OLD ADAGES ABOUT THE WEATHER

Adages are old sayings or proverbs used to pass down information from one generation to another. Before we had computer models and daily weather forecasts, people used adages based on patterns they observed in the weather to help them make predictions. Some adages are just superstitions, but some of them are based on science. Here are three old adages that hold their water.

SAYING: "If the goose honks high, fair weather. If the goose honks low, foul weather."

SCIENCE: Many birds fly higher when the weather is good and lower to avoid changes in air pressure or clouds.

SAYING: "When clouds appear like rocks and towers, the earth's refreshed with frequent showers."

SCIENCE: Some cloud types and shapes are indicators of rain, especially tall thunderheads.

SAYING: "Clear moon, frost soon."

SCIENCE: Clouds help trap stored heat from the ground at night. Clear skies release that heat into space, making for very cold mornings!

SIGNS OF CHANGE

· ·

Outside, you don't get a daily forecast, so the most local, reliable weather forecast comes from you. Learn to watch the weather closely for the small clues that a larger change is on the way. This means practicing looking up and around when you are outside: notice the sky, changes in the air, and what's moving and how fast. Here are some important signs of changes in the weather to watch for.

- Increases or decreases in air temperature
- Changes in light
- Increases or shifts in wind
- Changes in the shape, color, or elevation of clouds
- Thunder and lightning
- Hiding animals

TRY THIS! Make up adages that describe the weather where you live throughout the year. How do you know that a change is coming?

MEASURING THE WIND

Most new weather is brought in with the wind, so it's always been important for outdoorspeople to have a way to measure where the wind is coming from—and how fast.

Wind Direction

To measure wind direction, use a wind sock, vane, or the movement of leaves and small branches. For lighter winds, lick your finger and hold it up to determine which way the wind is blowing (the wetness helps you feel the breeze: whichever side feels colder is the direction the wind is coming from). When we talk about wind direction, we always talk about where the wind is coming from (upwind) instead of where it's going (downwind). An easy way to determine wind direction is to stand facing into the wind with your compass; the direction your compass points to is the wind direction.

Wind Speed

Modern weather stations are able to measure the speed of wind in miles or kilometers per hour; this is called a quantified measurement, one that gives us an actual number. Outdoors, though, it's not always possible to directly measure wind speed, so we make qualitative measurements, based on observations, to estimate what the wind speed might be. This helps us predict the timing of storms, how severe they might be, and what the *windchill* (what temperature it feels like if you are standing in the wind) will be.

In 1805, Francis Beaufort designed a scale of wind intensities based on observation, and by 1838, he had refined his scale so well that it was officially adopted by the English Royal Navy. The following is a *Girl's Guide* spin on Beaufort's scale.

THE *GIRL'S GUIDE* SCALE OF WIND INTENSITY

MILES PER HOUR	WEATHER NAME	OBSERVATIONS
Less than 1	Still	Smoke and steam rise straight up into the air.
1 to 4	Calm	Smoke and steam drift, but wind socks, vanes, or chimes do not.
4 to 7	Gentle breeze	You can feel the wind on your face. Leaves rustle. Wind socks, vanes, and chimes move.
7 to 12	Strong breeze	Leaves and small twigs are in constant motion. Flags and larger objects move a lot.
12 to 19	Light wind	Dust and loose paper move; small branches sway.
19 to 24	Wind	Small trees and medium branches start to sway; small waves appear on lakes.
24 to 31	Strong wind	Large branches move, the wind starts to make noise, telephone wires sway, and umbrellas are hard to use.
31 to 38	Stormy	Whole trees are in motion, and you have to brace against the wind.
38 to 46	Severe storm	Twigs break from trees, larger objects start to move, and it's difficult to walk. Time to take shelter!

TRY THIS! Use the rules for observation to guess the wind speeds on a windy day, and compare them to the weather report.

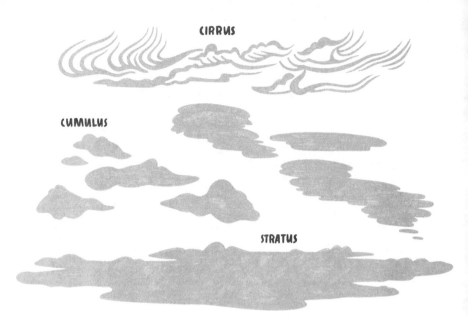

CIRRUS

CUMULUS

STRATUS

READING THE CLOUDS

Clouds are giant collections of tiny water and ice droplets
that form when evaporated water cools and condenses
in the air. Since clouds are carried by the wind, they are
another good way to determine wind direction. Fog is a
special kind of cloud that forms when cold, moist air gets
trapped near the ground. The size, shape, and behavior of
clouds can be clues to changing weather conditions.

- High, wispy *cirrus* clouds indicate rain in the next 12 to
  24 hours.

- *Lenticular*, or lens-shaped, clouds announce the arrival
  of precipitation to mountaintops.

- Tall, lumpy *cumulus* clouds produce summer thunder and lightning storms.

- Sheets of low, flat *stratus* clouds can rise, indicating fairer weather, or lower, indicating rain is on the way.

DID YOU KNOW? Clouds are white because the tiny water particles act like prisms, scattering all of the wavelengths of sunlight together to blend to white. When the particles are farther apart, the light waves scatter but don't mix, causing a rainbow to form.

THUNDER AND LIGHTNING

. . . .

Lightning is a giant electrical spark caused by the movement of charged rain particles inside a cloud. About one hundred lightning bolts strike the earth every second. Thunder is the sound of the air expanding as it is warmed by lightning. Thunder and lightning are most common on hot summer days and usually sound and look scarier than they are, but it's still not safe to be outside near lightning. If you *do* get caught in lightning:

- Stay low. Lightning often strikes the highest points, so move away from ridges and hilltops and crouch down.

- Stay buffered. Keep your pack or some other nonmetal material (like your shoes) between yourself and the ground.

- Ditch your metal. Metal attracts lightning, so drop metal stakes and poles before taking shelter; you can get them when the storm has passed.

Thunder and lightning start together but travel at different speeds. The longer there is between the lightning flash and the thunderclap, the farther they are from you.

TRY THIS! Count the seconds between lightning strikes and thunderclaps. Can you tell if the storm is getting closer or farther away?

Build Your Own Backyard Weather Station

Now that you know some things about the weather, you're ready to start making your own observations and forecasts by building your own backyard weather station with a thermometer, barometer, and rain gauge. This weather station can be placed or mounted anywhere outside, but try to find a place that is exposed to wind, rain, and sunshine and that you will be able to check regularly.

WHAT YOU'LL NEED:

Hot glue
Glue gun
1 outdoor thermometer
1 wood gardening stake
1 (6-inch) ruler
Scissors
1 (20-ounce) soda bottle
½ cup pebbles or small stones
Duct tape
Standard ruler
Permanent markers
Water
1 balloon
Craft glue
1 glass jar
Two rubber bands
2 plastic stir sticks or drinking straws
Clear tape
Weather log or field journal
Pencil

WHAT TO DO:

1. Choose a location for your station. Look for a place that is open to the weather and not likely to be disturbed.

2. With hot or craft glue, attach your thermometer to one side of the garden stake and the 6-inch ruler to the other, with "0" at the bottom. This will be the stand for your thermometer on one side and the gauge for your barometer on the other.

CONTINUED

3. For your rain gauge, cut the top off your 20-ounce bottle and place the stones in the bottom. Invert the cut-off top, put it inside the bottle funnel-end down, and attach it with glue, as in Build Your Own Fish Trap Viewer (page 52).

4. Cut a strip of duct tape slightly shorter than your bottle and attach it to the outside of the bottle lengthwise, from top to bottom, matching the bottom of the tape with the top of the stones.

5. Using a ruler and permanent markers, draw a line on the tape for each ¼ inch from the bottom to the top of the tape. Label each line.

6. Pour enough water into your rain gauge to just cover the rocks and line up with the base of your tape. This is your "zero" line. You will need to refill it every so often!

7. For your barometer, cut the neck off your balloon and run a thick coating of craft glue around the base of the jar neck.

8. Pull the balloon over the jar until it lies flat, making sure it forms a tight seal with the glue. Secure it with two rubber bands.

9. Tape the two straws together with clear tape to form one long straw.

10. Place a small glob of craft glue in the center of the balloon. Place one end of the straw into the glob so it lays horizontally, and cover with clear tape to hold it in place. This is your barometric needle. When the needle is in front of the 6-inch ruler attached to your stake, you can read increases and decreases in pressure by looking at the position of the straw in front of the ruler.

11. Get the help of an adult to secure your stake in the ground. Place your rain gauge to one side and your barometer to the other, making sure its needle reaches across your ruler.

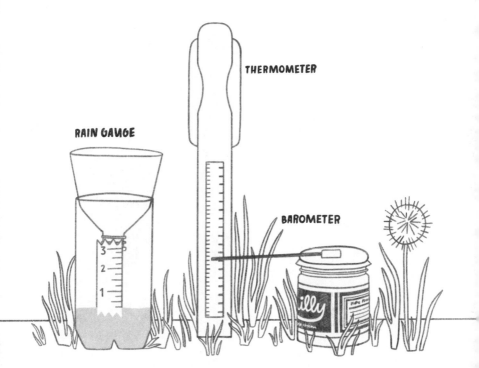

Record your observations and measurements in a weather log or field journal. Use your *Girl's Guide* Scale (page 165) and compass to record wind speed and direction. Read your barometer; has the needle gone up? Then so has the air pressure. If the straw needle has moved down or is low, the pressure has decreased. Look at the thermometer and read the temperature off the scale. Read the precipitation amount using the ruler along your gauge. Look around at the sky, and note if there are clouds and what kind you think they are. Look for other weather clues, like changes in light, dew, or animal behavior. Compare your measurements to your notes from the previous few days, taking into account what you know about the weather where you are at that time of year. Can you predict what the weather will do?

PSSSSSSST! Remember, when your barometer rises, it means colder weather is coming, while if it falls, warmer air is on the way.

HOW TO READ A MAP

Being able to read and use a map for navigation is one of the most important and fun outdoor activities. Most of us have phones or GPS that we can use to navigate, but it's important to know how to use a paper map because batteries run out, signals get lost, and sometimes online maps are not accurate, especially in wild areas.

A map is an overhead, shrunken-down picture of the land. There are maps that show countries, weather patterns, crops, and city streets. Outside, we use maps that show roads, trails, water, natural features, and hills and valleys (*topography*).

The first step in learning how to read maps is to look at a lot of them. Start by looking at maps of places you are already familiar with. Can you find your house on a map of your city? What kinds of shapes are used for buildings? Roads? Water? Think about those places in real life, and see how they look on paper. Learn to recognize the kinds of colors and symbols used for different things. Like anything else, navigation takes practice.

Navigation tools:

- Compass
- GPS and altimeter
- Small ruler
- Pencil

The Map Legend

Each map has its own coded language of shapes, colors, and symbols used to represent the real world. This map language is decoded on the *legend*. A legend is an area on the map that explains the symbols and provides other useful information. The legend shows you which kind of line marks trails and which marks roads, what pattern marks wetlands or forests, as well as what the symbols are for things like campgrounds or ranger stations. Always look at the legend before using any map, because not all maps use the same symbols.

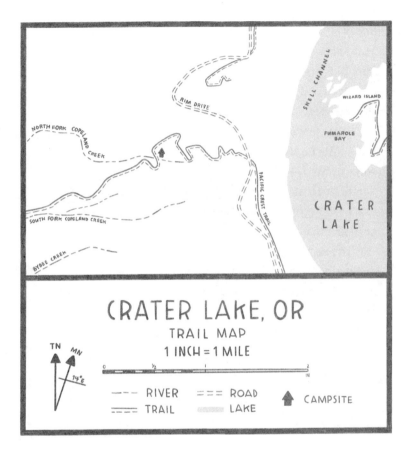

CRATER LAKE, OR
TRAIL MAP
1 INCH = 1 MILE

--- RIVER === ROAD ▲ CAMPSITE
=== TRAIL LAKE

Scale

Maps show you the same view you get from flying a drone. Just like the view from a drone, the higher up you are, the more you can see on your map. With computers, we call this zooming. In navigation, we call it *scale*.

Scale is what we use to determine distance on a map. Each mile on the ground may be represented by an inch or some other useful unit on the map. On that map, 10 miles would be 10 inches across the map. Scale is usually shown as a bar marked with distances and can always be found on or near the map legend.

To use a bar scale to figure out the distance of a path or the distance between two points, just use a stick, a piece of string, or your finger to mark off a mile (or some other useful distance), and then move it along the path or between the two things and add up the total.

Other ways to measure distance:

- Pedometers (these measure steps)
- Tachometers (these measure the working speed of an engine)
- Apps like MapMyWalk

HOW TO USE THE BAR SCALE

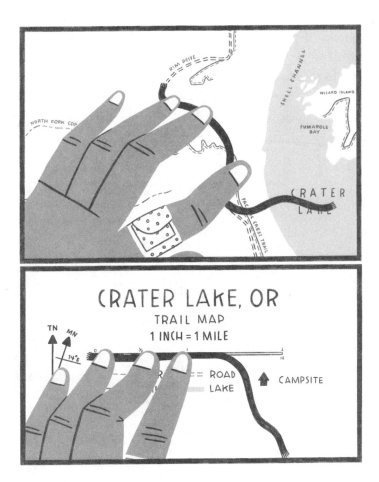

Direction

The first thing to do when navigating is line up the map with the real world. Use your compass and the four cardinal directions: north, south, east, and west. Every map is made with north at the top and east and west as right and left. The way to remember the order is the phrase "*n*ever *e*at *s*hredded *w*heat."

To find north in the real word, look at your compass needle or locate the North Star. When looking at a map, always try to match north in the real world with north on your map.

FINDING NORTH

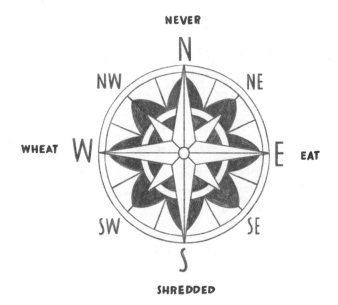

DID YOU KNOW? You can also find north by looking at where the sun is in the sky; the sun rises in the east and sets in the west.

A NOTE ON COMPASSES: The North Pole (true north) is not actually what your compass's north arrow points to. Compasses are drawn to the earth's magnetic pole, which is just a little off true north. The difference between true north and magnetic north is called *declination*. Before you can use your compass, you have to adjust it for declination (follow the directions that come with your compass). You can find the declination for your location on the legend of your map. Once you adjust your compass, it will point to true north.

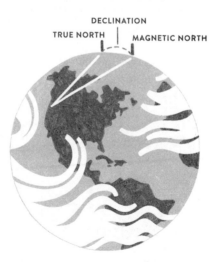

TRY THIS! Practice finding north in your day-to-day life. Is your home oriented to the cardinal directions? Which way does your head point when you are asleep in bed at night? Use landmarks, like your school or a park, to remember which way you are facing. Check your guesses with a compass.

You Are Here

Outside, it's important to always know where you are on the map and on the ground. You can find this out using your map, your observations, and your compass and with the help of a GPS and *altimeter*. Altimeters tell you your elevation—how high you are up a hill. A GPS will give you your coordinates in latitude and longitude—a global grid that helps you pinpoint your location. We read latitude vertically on a map and longitude across. Location coordinates are given in degrees, minutes, and seconds of latitude and longitude. Outside, pair your observations of the terrain with latitude and longitude to find your location on the map.

When you make observations to help find your location on a map, first orient yourself by facing the direction that the north arrows on both your map and your compass point to. Then look for the big stuff—notice the streams you cross, turns you make, and mountains, roads, or other large features that will be labeled on the map. Compare what you see in the real world to what you see on the map to find your location. See page 179.

Are We There Yet?

Knowing how fast you're going is important for navigation and trip planning, especially if you want to be back in time for dinner or before dark. If you want to know how fast you travel by foot, bike, boat, or any other means, take the total distance you've traveled and divide it by how long it took you. For example, if it took you 2 hours to walk 4 miles, that's 4 divided by 2, or 2 miles per hour!

Distance ÷ time = speed
4 miles ÷ 2 hours = 2 miles per hour

Calculate your speed several times in different conditions and locations (uphill, downhill, on sand, or on an easy path) to get a sense of how fast you generally travel. This is your average speed. Once you know your average speed, you can use that to estimate how long a hike, ride, or float will take. Just divide your total distance by the average speed.

Distance ÷ speed = time
6 miles ÷ 2 miles per hour = 3 hours

TRY THIS! Find mile markers on a trail, road, or track and time yourself walking a marked mile. Do this three times on different days at a medium pace to find out your average speed.

Hills and Valleys

Maps are flat, but the world is not. Sometimes the most important piece of information to have is what the land looks like. Are there hills? Valleys? Steep cliffs or rolling hills? These are important questions to ask when planning a route or finding your way. While most maps don't tell us that kind of information, topographic maps do, using lines of equal elevation we call *contour lines*. Contour lines are made by taking elevation measurements, plotting them on the map, and connecting all the points with the same elevation together, like connecting the dots.

Since every point on a contour line has the same elevation, if you walked along a path following a contour line on a map, you would never go up- or downhill. Lake edges are good examples of real-life contour lines.

HOW CONTOUR LINES ARE MADE

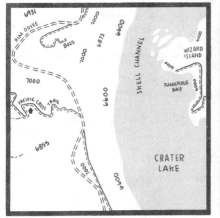 

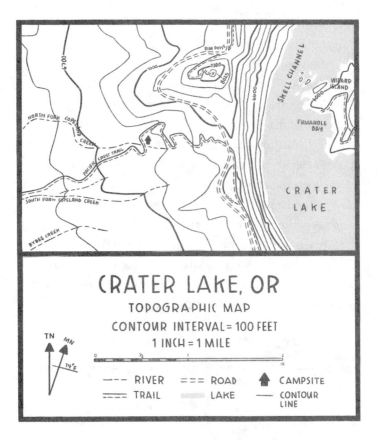

Usually, you will take a path that crosses contour lines. If the numbers go up, you're heading uphill. If they go down, you're going downhill. The amount you go up or down with each line is called the contour interval. You can find the contour interval of your map on the map legend.

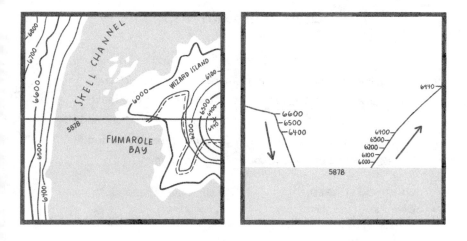

CHECKING YOUR WORK OUTSIDE

Whether you use a map or a GPS, it's still important to stop and consider whether the information on your device or map matches what you see around you in the real world. Does the map show you standing next to a lake, but you can't seem to see one? You might not be in the right place. Always stop every 20 minutes or so and check your map to make sure you know where you are.

If you do get turned around, and you're alone or in a group without an adult who knows what to do, stop where you are and instead focus on signaling for help with noise or light and keeping safe.

Draw Your Own Map

Most adventurers and explorers rely on maps they make themselves in addition to maps made by others, especially if they are in deep backcountry. Often the map you make yourself is the best one to rely on because it is current and shows the things you noticed or thought were interesting. Here's how to get started making your own maps.

WHAT YOU'LL NEED:
Compass (or use the sun!)
Measuring tape (or pace off
  your distances!)
Pencils, colored pencils,
  or markers
Ruler
Graph or plain paper

WHAT TO DO:

1. Using your compass or the sun, determine which way is north.

2. Determine the boundaries of your map in the real world. Use visible landmarks or sticks and stones to mark your map boundaries on the ground.

3. Measure the boundaries of your map in the real world using your measuring tape or by pacing it off.

4. Mark the boundaries on your paper map, showing your scale: 1 inch (or square if you're using graph paper) on the map is equal to how many feet in real life? Use an arrow to show which way is north.

5. Make a list of important features on your map: rocks, trees, streams, etc. Choose symbols or patterns to represent them.

6. Starting on one side of your map boundary in real life, walk and measure the distance from that boundary line to each feature. Turn, and repeat this process for each feature from another side. Now you have coordinates for each feature.

7. Mark the location of each feature on your map with a dot. Now measure the approximate size and shape of each feature and draw it to scale on your map.

8. Draw in and color or shade any other interesting or important features, such as grass, flower beds, dirt tracks, or pavement.

9. Make a legend for your map showing what symbols you used.

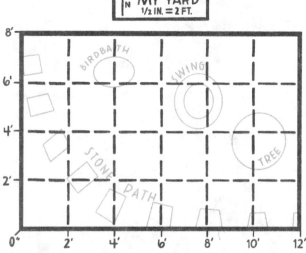

SACAGAWEA
The Navigator

Sacagawea was a Lemhi Shoshone girl, born around 1788, who led the Lewis and Clark expedition from Missouri to Oregon when she was just a teenager! She was responsible for navigating and interpreting during the 8,000-mile, 3-year-long expedition. She was an important ambassador for the otherwise all-male group, meeting with tribal leaders, forging relationships with them, and bartering for essential supplies wherever they went. She is also known as one of the most important natural historians of the time for her careful collection and observation of plants and animals throughout their journey. In 2000, the United States issued the Sacagawea dollar coin in her honor, close to 200 years after the expedition. That's a long time to wait for a little recognition!

Test Your Map Skills

Using the map on page 191, answer the following questions on a separate piece of paper:

1. One of the human-made things on the map is a _____.

2. Roads are shown as a) dotted lines; b) double dashed lines; c) double lines.

3. How tall is Owl Mountain?

4. Can you drive to Lake Swanee? Yes or no.

5. True or false: Chipmunk Creek runs north.

6. What direction would you travel if you were going from the fire lookout to the bridge on Chipmunk Creek? a) south; b) northeast; c) northwest.

7. How long is the Big Bear Trail in feet?

8. What is the contour interval?

9. What is the lowest place on the map?

10. If you go from *A* to *B*, are you a) going uphill; b) going downhill; c) staying level?

If you got between eight and ten answers right, congratulations! You're a map master!

If you got between five and seven answers right, good work! You're ready to go, but you still need some help from an experienced guide.

If you got fewer than five right, keep trying! Go back through this chapter and review before heading out.

QUIZ MAP

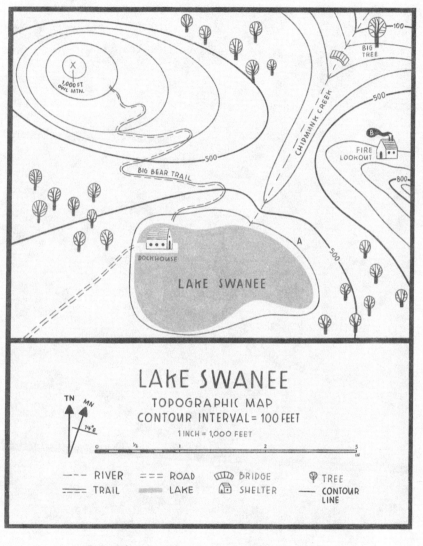

CHAPTER 9

SURPRISES AND MISHAPS

The other day, I met a bear,

A great big bear, a-way out there.

—CAMP SONG

One of the things that makes being outside exciting is the thrill of knowing that you are far away from home and relying mostly on yourself and your traveling companions. That's equally true in good weather, when everything is going perfectly, and on stormy days or when someone gets hurt. Knowing what to do and how to help turns challenges into adventures. Someday, you'll want to head out without a parent or group leader, so it's important to learn the skills of safety.

It's easy to stay safe if you remember these three basic rules:

1. Plan ahead.

2. Think before you act.

3. Stay alert.

This chapter is all about keeping out of, preparing for, and standing up to trouble.

BEFORE YOU GO

Stay safe by planning ahead. Make sure you do these things before you go:

- Memorize your adult leader's first and last name and phone number.

- If you are going on an adventure with just other kids, always tell a responsible adult where you are going and when you will be back.

- Keep a notecard in a plastic bag in your pack with emergency names and numbers, where you are staying, what kind of vehicle you arrived in, and any important medical information.

- Ask if there are rules for where you are going—and plan to follow them. They are there for a reason.

- Ask if there are hazards to avoid or special clothing or equipment you need to bring with you, and always bring your own essential items, like water and first-aid supplies (see Chapter 4: What to Bring, page 65).

DID YOU KNOW? In 1870, a blind man was lost for 37 days because of a lack of search-and-rescue services in what would become the United States' first national park—Yellowstone. Today, the National Park Service conducts over 2,500 search-and-rescue operations a year.

NIGHTTIME
· · · · · · · · · · · · · · · · · · ·

One of the first things you notice outside at night is how much darker it is without the glow from constant lights. It can be easy to tell yourself a scary story about what all might be lurking out there, but remember, most everything else has gone to bed too, and the things that are up at night? They're supposed to be out there. That rustling you hear is usually just a chipmunk or falling twig (or it might even be your little sister pulling a trick on you).

At camp, you can lighten things up with a campfire, lanterns (see Build Solar-Powered Mason Jar Lanterns, page 198), or the light from a full moon on a clear night. But even without those things, you can still rely on your natural *nocturnal* (night) tools. Your body has two ways it helps you see better in the dark. First, the pupil of your eye gets bigger to let in more light. Then your eye begins to collect *rhodopsin*, a special chemical that helps you to see shapes and movement in the dark. It can take up to 45 minutes for your eyes to fully adjust to the dark, but most of us start to see better in just a few minutes.

> **TRY THIS!** At home, use a clock or timer to see how long it takes for your eyes to adjust to the dark.

Tips for conquering your fear of the dark:

- Take a night hike. Face your fears and venture out on a familiar trail in the dark, with or without a flashlight (but definitely with an adult).

- Keep your flashlight handy. Stash one in a pocket and another one in your tent.

- Make it glow. Bring along your favorite light-up doo-hickey (like glow-in-the-dark wands, bands, balls, or clothing) to cast extra light in your tent all night long.

- Get *hyggelig* (pronounced "HOO-gah-lee") (see page 83). Make sure you are warm and comfortable enough to fall asleep, so you don't keep yourself up with worry.

Creatures of the Night

Humans aren't the only animals that like to stay up late. Nocturnal animals take advantage of the cover of darkness and cooler temperatures. A few of the animals most likely to be up and about in the middle of the night are:

- Owls
- Bats
- Possums, skunks, and raccoons
- Frogs and toads
- Cats

At night you can identify some animals by the color of their eye shine in light. Here's a handy guide to nighttime animal eye shine.

- Raccoon: bright yellow
- Opossum: orange
- Fox: white
- Deer: greenish white
- Cat: red

Build Solar-Powered Mason Jar Lanterns

Camp lanterns are usually designed for maximum illumination, which is great if you're trying to cook or set up camp after dark, but not so great if you just want some light to keep you from tripping on things at night. For a prettier (but still useful) illumination, try making these beautiful solar-powered lanterns.

WHAT YOU'LL NEED:
2 solar-powered lawn lights
Scissors
Ruler
Aluminum foil

2 glass mason jars (large enough to fit your lights)
2 mason jar lid rings (no lids)
Tissue paper of various colors
Clear-drying craft glue

WHAT TO DO:

1. Remove the plastic base from each of the solar lights.

2. Cut two (6-by-12-inch) pieces of foil, folding each in half to form a square.

3. Fit the foil squares snugly over the mouths of the jars, then gently screw on the rings.

4. With your scissors, cut an X (about the size of a quarter) in the foil. Gently poke the base of each light through the X. The solar panel should be up and outside the foil and the light should be down inside the jar.

5. To create a multicolor effect, tear, rip, or cut out pieces of tissue paper and glue them to the outsides of the jars.

6. Set out in the sun for several hours with the solar panels up to charge before using.

WHO ARE YOU? STRANGERS

Most of the time we spend outside is with friends, family, and troop members. In fact, one of the reasons outdoor activities are popular is because they give us a chance to spend time with our favorite people. Just like in your hometown, though, it's important to stay away from strangers in the wilderness.

How to be safe around strangers:

- Use the buddy system.
- Bring a dog.
- Look confident.
- Carry a whistle.
- Trust your instincts.
- Yell "no!" or "fire!" if you feel unsafe (these words can be heard clearly from long distances).
- Tell a trusted adult about the strangers.

If someone does approach you when you are by yourself outdoors, run as fast as you can toward the nearest camp, trailhead, road, or safe person—making as much noise as you possibly can.

> **TRY THIS!** Can you memorize three emergency phone numbers? It's important to be able to call for help using any available phone. Remember, if you're in the United States 911 usually only services developed areas, so look up the local sheriff's office number before you go.

Practice Yelling

Everyone always tells us to yell if we are in danger or there's another kind of emergency, but in the rest of our lives, they tell us we're not supposed to yell. And that's okay, until it's important to be good at yelling and you haven't practiced.

To fine-tune your skills, try yelling into a pillow as loud and as long as you can. Safety experts suggest yelling "fire" because it lets people know that there's an emergency. Try this several times, and you'll discover that it's really, really satisfying. When you've gotten good at it, try it someplace outside where no one will be disturbed—like at the beach.

Warning! It's best to let your folks know *before* you practice yelling.

BIG GAME

. . . .

Another thing people spend a lot of time talking about is running into dangerous animals outside. It's true, you might run into a bear, moose, snake, or mountain cat, but you're more likely to swat mosquitoes or lose a bag of chips to chipmunks than have to defend yourself from big game. Humans are noisy and stinky and usually wear brightly colored clothing, all of which lets most animals know we're coming a mile away.

Also, there are just not as many animals as there used to be. Humans use up a lot of land for cities, farms, and roads and that has made it hard for a lot of species to survive. While many wild animals are attracted to the smell of our food, most of them are more afraid of us than we are of them. If they do lash out by roaring or biting, which is rare, it's usually because they are scared, protecting their young, or you've accidentally gotten between them and their food. Everyone, especially bears, can get grumpy when they're hungry.

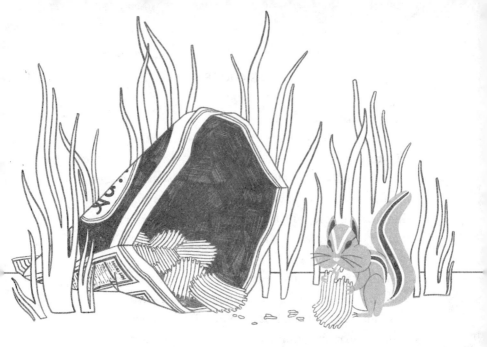

To avoid unwanted animal encounters of the not-so-scary kind (bugs and critters), keep all shelters, food, and gear tightly closed when not in use and be sure to inspect your shoes and clothes before you put them on for anything that might be trying to hitch a ride. In general, making a lot of noise, like clapping your hands or singing songs, is enough to make larger animals steer clear of people. If you do encounter an animal, here's what to do:

- Keep your distance.

- Leave it alone—this means don't feed it, poke it with a stick, or take selfies with it.

- Stop moving. Like most pets, wild animals take running as a sign that they should chase, so hold your ground.

- Get big. Most animals won't attack something bigger than themselves, so stand up tall, put your arms over your head, and clump with your group.
- Make noise. A loud shout or a sharp tone can often deter a big animal, so here's another good time to use your yell!
- Wait until the animal has left or lost interest before slowly backing away.

YOU ARE NOT A FISH! WATER SAFETY

Outdoor swimming is so much fun that sometimes it can be hard to remember that you are not a fish. You will still sink to the bottom if you jump in, you can't breathe underwater, and your body will not automatically adjust to the water temperature (which is almost sure to be cold!). With real water comes real risks: there are hidden rocks, drop-offs, and unpredictable currents, and the ocean can surprise you with an extra-big sneaker wave. But it's easy to have fun in the water as long as you follow a few simple guidelines.

Tips for enjoying a safe swim:
- Bring hiking sandals or water shoes to protect your feet.
- Swim in well-established swimming areas.
- Have an adult test the water depth and current conditions before you jump in.

- Keep an eye on the ocean—never turn your back to it.

- Wear a personal flotation device (life vest or life jacket).

Help keep others safe by learning how to spot distress. Real drowning doesn't look like it does on TV, with all the splashing and yelling. Most people in need of help in the water are quiet and still and sometimes look like they are climbing an invisible ladder. If you see someone you think might need help in the water, immediately tell an adult.

Remember, water safety starts with swim lessons, the more the better. The Red Cross offers swim lessons throughout North America for swimmers of all levels; find one near you!

FIRST AID

A good first-aid kit is the one you never have to use. But if you're outside having fun, you'll probably look down at the end of the day to see arms and legs covered with scratches, bumps, bruises, and bites. And on group trips, someone almost always needs at least a bandage.

First-Aid Kits

A first-aid kit is the one piece of gear that you probably have all the pieces for already lying around the house. Building your own kit is as easy as finding a sturdy ziplock or toiletry bag and labeling it with a bright-red cross.

What you'll need:

- Adhesive bandages and/or gauze of assorted sizes (for cuts and scrapes)
- Antiseptic wipes and antibiotic ointment (for cuts and scrapes)
- Ace bandage (for sprains)
- Medical gloves (for treating others)
- Tweezers (for splinters and stings)
- Burn gel (for burns)
- Moleskin (for hot spots and blisters)
- Antihistamine (for bites, stings, and allergies)
- Painkiller
- Personal medications or prescriptions
- Safety pins

Once your kit is packed, give it a permanent home in your backpack, where it can be easily found if you need it quickly or if someone else is looking for it. And remember to restock it every so often!

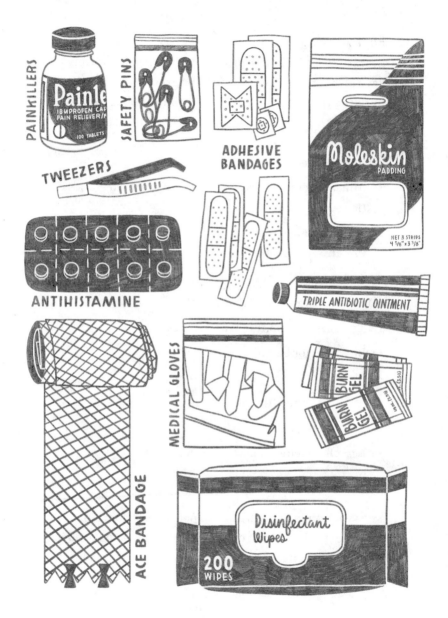

PAINKILLERS

SAFETY PINS

TWEEZERS

ADHESIVE BANDAGES

Moleskin PADDING

NET 3 STRIPS
4 5/8" x 3 3/8"

ANTIHISTAMINE

TRIPLE ANTIBIOTIC OINTMENT

MEDICAL GLOVES

BURN GEL

BURN GEL

ACE BANDAGE

Disinfectant Wipes

200 WIPES

How to Help

Even more important than having a first-aid kit is knowing how to use it, especially if you want to help a friend. Having first-aid training is part of being a good outdoor citizen. Outside we rely on one another to take care of most things that come up until we have a chance to get to help.

There should always be at least one person in the group who has first-aid training—usually the responsible adult. But sometimes you *are* the responsible person, like when you're in charge of younger kids or left alone for a time—so it's important to know how to treat some of the most common kinds of injuries. Besides, those responsible adults? They get sick or hurt too. And while there might be nothing funnier than watching your dad trip on a root, roll down a hill, and fall into an ice-cold stream, you'll still want to help him out when you stop laughing.

Talk to your troop leader or responsible adult *before* heading out about what to do if something happens to them. They will help you form a plan of action, just in case.

DID YOU KNOW? The Red Cross offers free and low-cost first-aid classes for kids, classes, and troops. Go to RedCross.org to find a class near you.

TRY THIS! Practice the two-person carry. With another "uninjured" friend, take up position near your "injured" friend's shoulders and feet. Lift under their arms and knees. For a more comfortable ride, make a bench seat by forming a square with your arms.

Common Problems

When you're outside, most of the time you'll run into the same things you would at home: bumps, scrapes, and maybe a splinter or two. Treat these common problems the same way you would at home, always remembering to keep your hands and the wound clean. When treating someone else, use medical gloves. Over the next few pages, you'll find solutions for handling common outdoor injuries and ailments.

SCRATCHES AND SCRAPES

Scratches and scrapes are common even at home, and we treat them about the same regardless of where we are. First, stop any bleeding by applying pressure with a clean towel or gauze. Once the bleeding is stopped, wash the wound with soap and water or rubbing alcohol, apply antibiotic ointment, and cover it with a bandage.

BURNS

Cooling is the key to treating burns. Cool, running water or a cold compress can be used on minor burns, but more severe burns will need an ice pack and burn gel. Always clean and cover burns after cooling them to help the skin heal. Remember, sunburns are just like any other burn, so treat them with cool water and aloe too!

DID YOU KNOW? People used to put everything from honey to pig fat on burns, which we now know can cause infection or even make the burn worse.

BUG BITES AND STINGS

The vast majority of the wildlife you see outdoors are bugs, and they are also the most likely to attack. We've all had bites and stings from bugs, so we know that most of them are harmless, but some bugs (like deer ticks and mosquitoes) carry disease, and others (like scorpions and some spiders) have bites that can be dangerous. You can treat most bites with calamine lotion or even just a cold compress, but if you get sick from a bite or have major swelling, it's time to head to a doctor. Avoiding getting bit in the first place is usually the best plan. Here's how:

- Avoid hives, mounds, and icky-looking water.
- Wear long pants and sleeves.
- Check your boots and sleeping bag before using them.
- Keep your tent door closed.
- Check your body, especially in nooks and crannies, for bites and ticks each day.

Bee stings can cause a serious allergic reaction, so if you carry an EpiPen, make sure that the people you are with know where it is and how to use it. You can treat a less exciting sting with ice and an antihistamine.

TRY THIS! Look up what kinds of poisonous bugs live in your area. Find out where they live and how to treat their bite or sting.

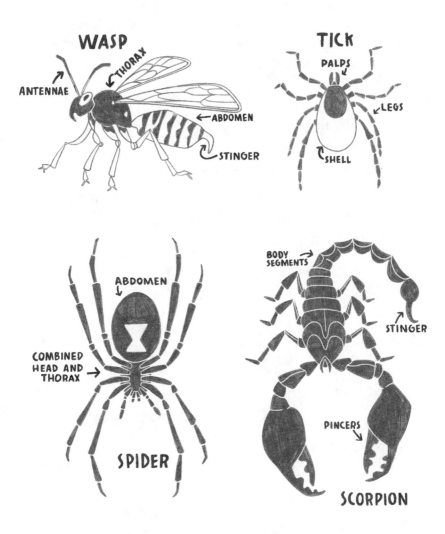

SPRAINS

A sprain is the stretching or breaking of the tendon—the stretchy bit that holds your joints together—often associated with rolling an ankle. It is super painful. You will know that you have sprained an ankle because it will hurt a lot, swell up, and maybe even turn purple. Sprains should be treated immediately by using *R-I-C-E*: rest, ice, compression, and elevation.

To wrap an ankle:

1. Wrap the bandage once around the ball of your foot, then diagonally across the arch until you reach your heel.

2. Skipping your heel, wrap from the base of your ankle to just above the knobby bit.

3. Secure the bandage with Velcro or clips.

STEP 1

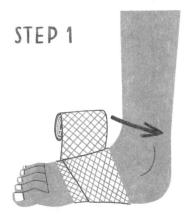

STEP 2

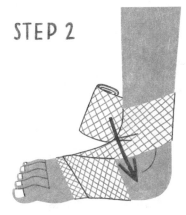

STEP 3

FINISHED WRAP

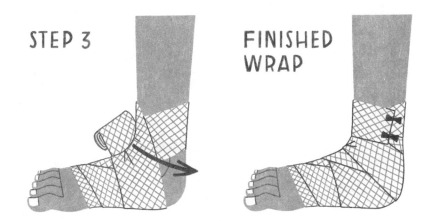

- White/cream berries
- White flowers in groups of six
- Hairy vines
- Leaflets* come to a point at the end

POISON IVY

- Greenish-tan berries
- White flowers in groups of six
- Leaflets* have a shine and can be slightly hairy

POISON OAK

- Grow as large as a shrub or tree
- Multiple leaflets* (usually five to thirteen), always an odd number
- Leaf resembles a feather

POISON SUMAC

*Leaflets can be green, yellow, or red depending on season

POISONOUS PLANTS

Some plants are serious about being left alone. So serious, in fact, that they have developed major defenses, like thorns and nettles. Other plants secrete oils and other substances that cause rashes and sores on humans. The most common poisonous plants are poison ivy, poison oak, and poison sumac, and they are all pretty easy to avoid once you know how to identify them. Before you head out, ask the ranger or locals if there are any poisonous plants around, and if so, have them point them out to you. If you do get exposed, use an over-the-counter ointment designed to treat these rashes or simple Dawn dish soap to wash the oil away. Remember, the best way to avoid poisonous plants is to stay on the trail!

THIN AIR

As you go uphill from sea level, the amount of oxygen in the air decreases, but your body still needs the same amount. If you go too high up in elevation too quickly—like when you climb a mountain—you can get altitude sickness from the lack of oxygen. Headaches, dizziness, and a hard time breathing are all signs of altitude sickness—generally, it makes you feel like a fish out of water.

Since going up is how you get altitude sickness, it makes sense that the way to fix it is by going down—fast! If you or someone in your group thinks they might have altitude sickness, try to go downhill at least 1,000 feet in elevation before resting to see how you or they feel.

TOO HOT AND TOO COLD

Hypothermia is what happens when you get *way too cold,* so cold that your body has a hard time working properly. Hypothermia is common when people fall into cold water or are outside in freezing temperatures without the right protection. You can avoid hypothermia by eating enough food, wearing warm clothing, and moving around a lot.

Someone with severe hypothermia might shiver a lot, have a hard time walking around, and be confused. They will need medical attention, but it's not good to try to move someone who is hypothermic, so while one person goes for help, have another person work on keeping the hypothermic person as warm as possible. This means getting them dry if they are wet, protecting them from the wind, covering them with as many blankets and clothes as you can find, and snuggling in next to them to share warmth.

The opposite of hypothermia is *heat exhaustion* or the more serious version, *heat stroke.* Heat exhaustion and stroke happen when your body gets too hot—remember, we like to be a steady 98.6 degrees Fahrenheit. People who are overheated may actually have cool, dry skin, since their heat isn't escaping with sweat, and they may complain of an upset stomach, cramping, or a headache. They can also get really crabby and irritable, so don't take it personally. Help an overheated person by finding a cool place in the shade for them to sit, giving them a damp cloth for their head, and giving them water to drink.

DID YOU KNOW? The hottest temperature ever recorded on earth was in Death Valley, California, in 1913. The record high for that day was a whopping 134 degrees Fahrenheit! The coldest place in the United States is Fairbanks, Alaska, where the average yearly temperature can be as low as -17 degrees Fahrenheit.

KNOW YOUR LIMITS

Everyone has a limit, and sometimes there are things that we just don't want to do. Maybe we already know it isn't safe, maybe it involves breaking a rule, or maybe there's just a little voice telling us not to. When it comes to safety, go with your gut. If you don't think something's safe, or if it's just not a challenge that you're up to, find your voice and use it. There's no reason you can't hang out and watch or stay at camp and read. Besides, pushing yourself too far and getting sick or hurt because of it is miserable for everyone. It's okay to sit something out.

Just as important as honoring your limits is honoring the limits of others—peer pressure is never cool, especially if someone gets hurt.

If something does go wrong, stay calm, think before you act, and above all, stay positive!

CLARA BARTON
Founder of the American Red Cross

Clara Barton was born in 1821 in Oxford, Massachusetts, and was one of only a few girls able to go school at that time, because her parents thought education for girls was just as important as education for boys. She started early, following her older brother to school at just 3 years old! Clara started nursing when she was 10, after her brother was badly injured falling from a barn roof. Even though doctors gave up on him, Clara persisted, and after many years she was able to nurse him back to health. At only 17 she became a schoolteacher, and in 1853 she opened the first free school in New Jersey. When the Civil War began, Clara used her knowledge of nursing to care for the soldiers on the battlefield and worked with other women to gather, store, and distribute medical supplies wherever they were needed. After the war, Clara formed the American Red Cross—an organization that provides care to people during emergencies and disasters. Now, the American Red Cross helps someone in the United States every 8 minutes.

Check Your Safety Skills

How prepared are you to head into the outdoors? Take the quiz below to find out if your safety skills are up to snuff. Remember to use a separate piece of paper, so you can take the quiz again if you need to review.

1. If you get too hot, a) keep moving to create a breeze; b) eat something; c) find shade and drink water.

2. The best way to avoid poison plants is to a) hike off trail; b) wear shorts; c) know how to identify them.

3. Water usually looks a) deeper and faster than it is; b) just as it is; c) shallower and calmer than it really is.

4. If you see a bear, a) run; b) play dead; c) get big and make noise.

5. The three basic rules of safety are to plan ahead, think first, and a) stay positive; b) stay alert; c) stay awesome.

6. Outside, it's okay to talk to strangers who a) are friendly; b) offer you candy; c) are rangers or camp hosts.

7. Dehydration is caused by lack of a) oxygen; b) water; c) electrolytes.

8. True or false: You can get hypothermia only in the snow.

9. One of the things you can do to treat an ankle sprain is a) walk around on it; b) soak it in warm water; c) wrap it with an ace bandage.

10. One of the ways to treat a burn outside is with a) cool, running water; b) bacon grease; c) sunscreen.

ANSWER KEY: 1. c; 2. c; 3. c; 4. c; 5. b; 6. c; 7. b; 8. false; 9. c; 10. a

THINGS TO LOOK FOR

Down by the banks of the Hanky Panky,

Where the bullfrogs jump from bank to banky.

—CLAPPING GAME

There's so much to see outside that knowing how to look and what to look for are their own set of skills. What's the difference between those two birds? What kinds of rocks are in that stream? Is that a star or a planet? This chapter is all about how to discover the most about what you find outside, from plants to planets.

Tips for making observations:

- Use more than one of your senses: look, listen, smell, and touch.
- Be still and quiet.
- Take your time.
- Notice what isn't there.
- Ask why.
- Look from up close and far away.

Tools for field exploration:

- Notebook or field journal/log and pencil
- Camera
- Magnifying glass
- Fish trap (see Build Your Own Fish Trap Viewer, page 52), butterfly net, or collection jar
- Binoculars or telescope

TRY THIS! Practice making observations. Can you make ten different observations about a single plant, animal, or rock? Start with things like color, feel, and smell. Then ask yourself—is it:

- Big?
- Small?
- Loud?
- Natural or human-made?
- Stinky?
- Shiny or transparent?
- Moving or still?
- Colorful?
- Alive?
- Working or playing?
- Made of many parts?
- In air or water?
- In a group or all alone?
- Near or far?
- Rough, smooth, or sticky?

TREES

· · · · · · · · · · · ·

There are two basic kinds of trees: conifers and broad-leaved trees. Conifer trees, such as pines, typically have needles and stay green throughout the year. Broad-leaved trees grow leaves and shed them each fall. There are more than 650 native tree species in North America.

CONIFER　　　　　　　　　　　**BROAD-LEAVED**

　Overall silhouette　

　Needle or leaf shape　

　Bark texture　

　Flowers
Fruit
Seeds

DID YOU KNOW? Palm trees aren't really trees. Instead of being woody, palm-tree trunks are made of tightly bound grasses.

TRY THIS! Make tree-ring or bark rubbings using thin paper and crayons. Can you determine the tree's age by counting its rings?

PLANTS AND WILDFLOWERS
. . . .

Every type of ecosystem (forest, grassland, etc.) has its own unique *assemblage* (group) of plants that thrive there. In fact, there are tens of thousands of plants and wildflowers that grow just in North America. The most important plants for outdoor adventurers to be able to identify are the ones to avoid, like poison ivy, oak, or sumac (see page 216). Start by learning the names and characteristics of the plants that live near you.

Things to look for:

- Leaf and petal arrangement
- Leaf shape
- Leaf texture (fuzzy, oily, etc.)

- Stem color and texture
- Color
- Berries
- Fragrance

TRY THIS! Collect samples of your favorite wildflowers and press them using parchment paper and two heavy books. Once dry, mount them between contact paper to preserve them.

DID YOU KNOW? Some plants are carnivorous. The *Darlingtonia californica*, or cobra lily, found along the west coast of the United States, eats insects by luring them into a chamber filled with sweet nectar.

MUSHROOMS

Fungi are their own kingdom of living things. Like plants, they produce a fruit, or mushroom, that they use to reproduce. Unlike plants, which make their own food by converting light, water, and carbon dioxide into sugars, fungi hunt for and absorb nutrients from their environment, like animals. Some mushrooms are edible, but you should never eat wild mushrooms unless they have been picked by an expert.

Things to look for:

- Cap and stem

- Color

- Grouping (clusters, lines, or circles)

- Gills

TRY THIS! Sketch some of your favorite mushrooms in your field journal. Using an ink pad, make a stamp of the bottom of the mushroom cap. You can use this spore print to help you identify your sample.

CHANTERELLES

TOADSTOOLS

Create a Time-Based Art Project

The natural world is always changing; plants grow, flowers open, skies shift, and rocks erode away. Most of these changes happen either too quickly or too slowly for humans to observe. One way to see the action is to use *time lapse*. Time lapse is the method of capturing images, videos, or sounds over several periods of time (for example, once a day for a month), and bringing them together to show how your subject has changed over time. Want to show how a tree changes with the seasons? Take a picture of it from the same location every week for a year. Want to show how a sunflower moves to follow the sun? Take a picture of it from the same angle every daylight hour over the course of a single day. To look at or listen more closely to fast-moving things like fish, birds, or water, consider slowing down your recording. Do the project with friends and then create a gallery show at the end to exhibit your work.

THINGS TO USE:
Camera
Video camera
Sound recorder
Drawing pad and colored pencils

WHAT TO DO:

1. Choose your subject.

2. Choose your medium (photographs, sketches, sound recordings, etc.).

3. Choose your time interval (seconds, hours, days, weeks).

CONTINUED

4. Set up your captures, or shots. Make sure you can return to the same location more than once.

5. Choose a way to compile your images or sounds—in a video, flip book, audio recording, or visual timeline.

6. Edit your material (make it go faster or slower).

7. Present your project to friends, family, or troop members.

ANIMALS

In spite of all the bear canisters, food hanging, hole digging, and general "watch out fors," seeing animals is a big part of why most of us like to spend time outdoors. Here are some tips for how to see the wildlife in your area:

- Stay quiet.

- Wear colors that help you blend in or hide.

- Choose a location where animals sleep or eat.

- Watch in the morning and early evening hours, when most animals are active.

DID YOU KNOW? More than five thousand elk bed down for the winter in the National Elk Refuge near Grand Teton National Park in Wyoming. That's nearly half the population of Jackson Hole, the nearest town!

Signs of life:

- Tracks and/or prints
- Scat (poop)
- Calls and/or sounds
- Scratches in dirt or on trees
- Pellets and fur balls

- Trails, dens, and burrows
- Broken or chewed vegetation and trees
- Homes: nests, webs, grassy beds

TRY THIS! Keep a page of your field journal just for animal sightings. List the date and location where you saw each animal, what it was doing, and any other observations you can make.

Insects

Insects are found almost everywhere on earth, and there are more kinds of insects than there are any other kind of animal. All insects have six legs and a body made of three sections: head, abdomen, and thorax. Most, but not all, insects also fly.

Things to look for:

- Colors
- Number of legs
- Body segments
- Antennae
- Wings

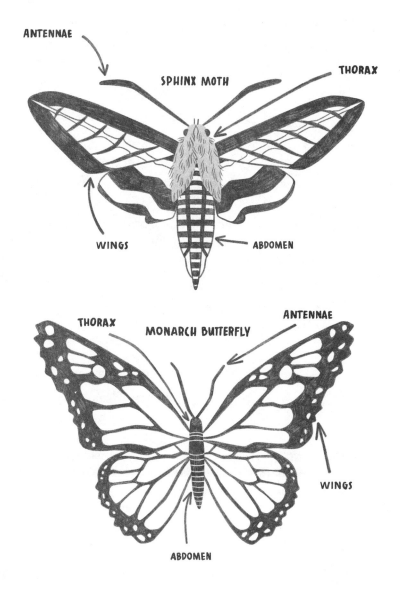

ANTENNAE

SPHINX MOTH

THORAX

WINGS

ABDOMEN

THORAX

MONARCH BUTTERFLY

ANTENNAE

WINGS

ABDOMEN

Birds

After insects, birds are the most commonly sighted type of wildlife. There are over nine thousand bird species worldwide. You can watch for birds from any location, even your own home. Many types of birds migrate south to warmer areas in the winter and north in the summer—this means you can see different kinds of birds throughout the year. In most bird species, the male is more brightly decorated than the female.

Things to look for:

- Size
- Shape
- Colors

- Call
- Plumage (feathers)
- Beak and feet features

BIRDCALLS

Sometimes you don't even need to see birds to be able to identify them. All bird species have their own special calls and responses. Here are some of the most recognizable.

- Barred owl: deep *who-who-who*
- Chickadee: light *chicka-dee-dee-dee*
- Ravens and crows: high-pitched squawking
- Seagulls: lingering *coo-ahhh*

DID YOU KNOW? If you hear a bird at night, it is almost always an owl, but nightingales, mockingbirds, and whip-poor-wills are also known for their night calls.

TRY THIS! Join thousands of bird-watchers for the National Audubon Society's annual Christmas Bird Count, the longest-running citizen-science bird project. They have been counting North American birds for more than 100 years! Find out more at Audubon.org.

ROCKS

Living things make up only a small percentage of the planet. The rest of the earth is made up of water, rocks, and minerals. There are three basic kinds of rocks: igneous (volcanic), sedimentary, and metamorphic. Volcanic rocks are made from the molten interior of the earth (lava). Sedimentary rocks are made of fragments of other rocks held together with natural cements, like sandstone. All of the world's fossils are found in sedimentary rocks. Rocks that have been pushed, pulled, or heated up so much that they have turned into different rocks entirely are metamorphic. Bring a shovel, rock hammer, pail, and sifter with you to help you dig, carry, and sort your rock specimens and a magnifying glass or hand lens to look at them up close.

Things to look for:

- Holes
- Crystals
- Fragments of other rocks
- Layers
- Folds
- Colors
- Texture

- Shine (luster)
- Hardness (Can you scratch it with a fingernail? Or a real nail?)
- Transparency
- Magnetism (Does it attract a magnet?)

DID YOU KNOW? Dinosaurs lived more than 65 million years ago, so everything we know about them we learned from fossils. The first complete dinosaur skeleton was found in New Jersey in 1848.

TRY THIS! Collect one small rock or a jam jar of soil (or sand) from every place you travel. Label and display them on a windowsill or shelf. How are they different or the same? Can you identify each one? Keep a record of your finds in your field journal.

THE NIGHT SKY

Just because the sun goes down doesn't mean there isn't anything interesting to look at. The night sky is full of things to observe, from the *aurora borealis* (northern lights) to the annual Perseid meteor shower.

Stars are balls of hot gases called *plasma*. Every star is a sun, and there are billions of them. The evidence for this is the Milky Way, our own galaxy, which often looks like a fuzzy band across the sky but on especially clear nights you can see is made up of stars. Constellations are groupings of stars that form sky pictures. They were made up thousands of years ago by early stargazers, poets, astronomers, and sailors to help them visualize and understand the patterns and changes of the night sky. Modern astronomers still use constellations to help navigate the sky. There are eighty-eight official constellations.

TRY THIS! Look up at the sky and pick out a few stars to make up your own constellation, giving it a name and a story. Draw a picture connecting the dots of the stars. Come back 3 nights in a row to see if you can still find it!

Tips for viewing the night sky:

- Cover your flashlight with red cellophane or cloth to preserve your night vision.
- Find a place with an open view, away from city lights.
- Turn your back to the moon.
- Lie down for extended viewing so your neck doesn't get stiff.

CYGNUS

CASSIOPEIA

MARY ANNING
Fossil Finder

Mary Anning was a pioneer of *paleontology* (the study of fossils), even though she grew up in a poor family in the south of England, never traveled the world, and wasn't allowed into the Geological Society of London because she was a girl. Mary's knowledge of fossils grew from her near-daily walks along the sea cliffs near her home. She found the first prehistoric fossils in the early 1800s, and scientists from around the world came to see her collection and learn from her. Her fossil collection became so famous that she became the inspiration for the tongue twister, "She sells seashells by the seashore."

ALL'S WELL THAT ENDS WELL
Protecting the Outdoors

The outdoors is more than just a place to play, adventure, and learn; it's home to all the world's plants and animals and is the only source of our clean water, wood, oil, medicines, and other natural resources. It's important that if you enjoy or use the natural world, you also help care for and preserve it for future generations.

Things you can do to protect nature while you're outside:

- Stay on the trail.
- Pack out garbage and litter.
- Reduce noise and light pollution.
- Do no damage.
- Follow posted rules, especially about fire.
- Leave no trace.
- Take nothing but pictures.

TRY THIS! Keep an extra garbage bag in your pack just for collecting litter as you go.

Things you can do to protect nature *every day*:

- Conserve water.

- Reduce, reuse, and recycle.

- Plant a tree.

- Create backyard habitat for birds, butterflies, and other creatures.

- Walk, bike, ride share, or use public transportation.

- Support a local conservation group.

- Write a letter to a lawmaker to urge them to protect nature.

TRY THIS! If you're in the United States, write or call your senator, representative, or the president to tell them to protect wild areas in your state. For the president of the United States, go to WhiteHouse.gov or call 202-456-1111. For a member of the House of Representatives, call 202-225-3121. To call your senators, dial 202-224-3121. You can find e-mails for American elected officials at USA.gov. If you're located elsewhere, look online for the contact information for your local government.

ACKNOWLEDGMENTS

This book would not have been possible without the help and support of the indispensable Hannah Elnan, the amazing people at Sasquatch Books, and the supremely talented Teresa Grasseschi. Special thanks is owed to Riley Hampshire for helping to design and test the projects and Noa Roxborough for essential perspective and insight. Many thanks as well to Kenya Luvert, Taevian Montgomery Bolds, Caroline Paul, Jeff Geiger, Suzi Steffen, Isha Rose Marin, and Jim and Pat McConnell for their advice, friendship, and wisdom. Most of all, I'd like to thank camp counselors, troop leaders, and outdoor educators everywhere—it works!

RESOURCES

CHAPTER 1: PLACES NEAR AND FAR

ON PUBLIC LANDS:
FS.fed.us
NPS.gov

ON WORLD HERITAGE SITES:
http://whc.unesco.org/en/list/
The Oldest Living Things in the World, Rachel Sussman, 2014

ON THROUGH TRAILS:
PCTA.org
www.appalachiantrail.org/about-the-trail

ON ARUNIMA SINHA:
http://arunimasinha.com/

CHAPTER 2: GROUPS, TROOPS, AND SISTERHOODS

ON DICE AND GAMING:
According to Hoyle, Richard L. Frey, 1969

ON JULIETTE GORDON LOW:
Junior Girl Scout Handbook, Girl Scouts of America, 1963

CHAPTER 3: OUTDOOR PURSUITS

ON HOLDING YOUR BREATH:
www.guinnessworldrecords.com/

ON LIBBY RIDDLES:
LibbyRiddles.com

CHAPTER 4: WHAT TO BRING

ON MOTHS:
Peterson First Guide to Butterflies and Moths of North America,
Paul A. Opler, 1998
www.nature.com/news
/moth-smashes-ultrasound-hearing-records-1.12941

CHAPTER 5: MAKING YOUR HOME AWAY FROM HOME

ON *HYGGE*:
www.visitdenmark.com/hygge

ON OUTDOOR SHELTERS:
Shelters, Shacks, and Shanties, Daniel Carter Beard, 1920

ON BUILDING FIRES AND FIRE REGULATIONS:
www.fs.fed.us/visit/know-before-you-go/fire

ON FIRE SAFETY:
www.nps.gov/fire

ON CLARE MARIE HODGES:
https://www.adventure-journal.com/2018/05/historical
-badass-claire-marie-hodges-first-female-national-park
-ranger/

CHAPTER 6: GOOD GRUB

ON SEAWATER:
http://oceanservice.noaa.gov/facts/drinksw.html

ON FANNIE FARMER:
www.notablebiographies.com/Du-Fi/Farmer-Fannie.html

CHAPTER 7: GIRL STUFF

ON ANIMALS STORING WATER:
http://mentalfloss.com/article/57204/20-amazing-animal
-adaptations-living-desert
www.bbc.com/earth/story/20160926-the-creatures-that
-can-survive-without-water-for-years

ON JUDY BLUME:
JudyBlume.com

CHAPTER 8: MAPS AND WEATHER

ON WEATHER:
Basic Essentials: Weather Forecasting, 3rd edition, Michael
Hodgson, 2007
NOAA.gov

ON THE BEAUFORT SCALE OF WIND INTENSITY:
http://weather.mailasail.com/Franks-Weather
/Historical-And-Contemporay-Versions-Of-Beaufort-Scales

ON LIGHTNING:
www.nssl.noaa.gov/education/svrwx101/lightning/faq/

CHAPTER 9: SURPRISES AND MISHAPS

ON STRANGERS AND PERSONAL SAFETY:
KidSmartz.org

ON FIRST-AID CLASSES AND CLARA BARTON:
RedCross.org

CHAPTER 10: THINGS TO LOOK FOR

ON TREES:
Spotter's Guide to Trees of North America, Alan Mitchell, 1993
Trees of North America: A Guide to Field Identification, C. Frank
Brockman, 2001

ON INSECTS:
My First Pocket Guide: Insects, Daniel J. Bickel, 2001

ON BIRDS:
Smithsonian Kids' Field Guides: Birds of North America East, Jo
S. Kittinger, 2001
Smithsonian Kids' Field Guides: Birds of North America West, Jo
S. Kittinger, 2001
The Young Birder's Guide to Birds of Eastern North America, Bill
Thompson III, 2008

ON WILDFLOWERS:
National Audubon Society First Field Guide: Wildflowers, Susan
Hood, 1998

ON ROCKS:
Discover More: Rocks and Minerals, Dan Green, 2013

ON THE SKY:
National Audubon Society First Field Guide: Night Sky, Gary
Mechler, 1999
Night Science for Kids: Exploring the World After Dark, Terry
Krautwurst, 2003

ON *DARLINGTONIA CALIFORNICA*:
http://oregonstateparks.org/index.cfm?do=parkPage
.dsp_parkPage&parkId=81

ON ELK:
https://www.fws.gov/refuge/national_elk_refuge/

ON SIGNS OF LIFE:
Animal Tracks and Signs, Jinny Johnson, 2008

ON MARY ANNING:
http://www.ucmp.berkeley.edu/history/anning.html

SONG LYRICS AND MUSIC

ScoutSongs.com
UltimateCampResource.com

INDEX

I

icebreaker games, 25–26
I Doubt It (card game), 31
Ingalls Wilder, Laura, *80*, 81
injuries. *See* first aid
insect bites and stings,
    211–213, *212*, *213*
insects, observing, 232–234,
    233

J

Jasper National Park
    (Canada), 10, *12*
journals. *See* field journals
junoon (passion), 19

K

karst, 14
Kick the Can (game), 31
knot tying, 94, *94*

L

land sports, 44–46, *45*
Lanterns, Solar-Powered
    (project), 198–199, *199*
leg cramps, 153
legend, map, 174, *175*
lenticular clouds, 166
lightning, 167–168
logs. *See* field journals
Low, Juliette Gordon, *36*, 37

M

makeup, 142
mancala (game), 27
Mancala Board project,
    28–29, *28*
mangrove ecosystem, 9
maps, 173–191
    Drawing Your Own Map
        (project), 186–187, *187*
    geocaching and orienteer-
        ing, 58
    learning how to read,
        173–185
    national parks, *6–7*
    quiz for testing your skills,
        190, *191*
    World Heritage sites, *12–13*
measurements and standards,
    cooking, 116–117
Memory (game), 26–27
menstruation, 149–151
moths, 232, *233*
mountain biking, 44
mountain climbing, *18*, 19, 54
Mount Fuji (Japan), 11, *13*
muscle soreness, 153
"mushing." *See* dogsledding
mushrooms, 228, *228*

N

Name game, 26
national parks and forests,
    4–9, *104*, 105
    map, *6–7*
nature, observations of,
    223–245

ABOUT THE AUTHOR

RUBY McCONNELL is a writer, geologist, and environmental advocate. She is a proud daughter of Oregon country. You can almost always find her in the woods. Follow her on Twitter and Instagram @RubyGoneWild and at RubyMcConnell.com.

ABOUT THE ILLUSTRATOR

TERESA GRASSESCHI is an illustrator, painter, and lifelong glasses wearer who spends her days making pictures for books, brands, and galleries. Her work has been featured in publications such as *Stereogum, Rolling Stone,* and the *Wall Street Journal*. This is her first book for children. She lives in Seattle, Washington. Follow her on Instagram @TeresaGrasseschi.